Journals
of
faith

BEAUTY FOR ASHES

DAVINA CASSELL

Journals

of

faith

BEAUTY FOR ASHES

In memory of Grandma Rosa Lee Long

Contents

Introduction

This book, *Journals of Faith*, was birthed from a collection of my personal writings and audio recordings, spanning a ten-to-twelve-year period; some date back to as early as 2009. These started off as casual writings and impromptu recordings that ultimately increased my faith and helped me to see things through God's Word. I had to journalize my faith, meaning I had to either write it on paper or speak it out loud to myself. I would grab my cell phone and audio-record events as they unraveled right in front of me. Some recordings or writings were after the fact, as I sought the scripture that spoke to my situation. I had to encourage myself, and the Word of God was my solution. I found recording very helpful as I meditated on God's Word and the Lord ministered to my spirit at that moment. Years later, I collected my handwritten journals, some from a book and some from scrap paper in a desk drawer, along with my transcribed audio recordings; this became what I call *Journals of Faith*. I am truly amazed; the purpose was to encourage myself, and now my prayer is that these journals of faith encourage you.

I gained so much joy, faith, love, and hope from the Word of God. At the top of each page is a scripture that I meditated on; it encouraged me and helped me to continue to move forward in faith and trust in God. I encourage you to journalize your own faith as you meditate on God's Word.

Keep the faith and meditate on God's Word daily. Follow His instructions in life, and you will succeed. As you stroll through life, take heed of life principles and the Word of God. The Word of God comes to teach us what is right and wrong in our lives. Over a decade, I have come to know the Word of God, and it is true and teachable. It will guide you, protect you, comfort you, give you strength, and give you hope for tomorrow. As we experience tough times or hardships of the world, we nevertheless must trust in God. Stay close to His Word. For every situation in life that you experience, the answer is in the Bible. I pray that these testimonies—inscriptions from my own faith journal—will inspire you, increase your faith, or help you to overcome the evil one. Revelation 12:11 states, and they overcame him [the devil] by the blood of the Lamb, and by the word of their testimony.

Beauty for Ashes
Davina

God Is with You

"But the Lord was with Joseph and showed him mercy, and He gave him favor in the sight of the keeper of the prison." Genesis 39: 21 (NKJV)

Never doubt whether the Lord is with you. There may come a time that everything in your life will make you feel like the Lord is not with you, but He is! Never forget that.

I read in the Old Testament about Joseph, Jacob's son, who was sold into slavery to Potiphar's house (an Egyptian officer). The Bible says the Lord was with him even then, giving him success in all he did. And while he was there, Potiphar made him in charge of everything, and everything flourished, blessed by Joseph's hand.

Prior to Joseph being sold into slavery, his brothers disliked him and were jealous of him. At first, they thought of killing him, but they figured that was too harsh and decided to put him in a pit instead. It was horrible what his own family did to him. Now, can you imagine things happening to you out of your control and you feeling lost, hurt, or abandoned? But all along, the Lord was with Joseph, and He is with you.

This is what we must realize, despite what we go through. This goes along with our faith. No matter what we see and what we feel, we must walk by faith. Regardless of how horrible things are or unexplainable, trust God. He is with you.

I recall looking at situations in my own life and questioning why that happened to me and why people treated me as they did. I began to think it was something I did, and the Lord was not pleased with me. But you know, sometimes things happen, and we just do not know and will never understand the why. That does not mean the Lord is not with you.

The Bible says hope deferred makes the heart sick, and sometimes it really does, in my experience. At one point, I had these highs and lows, and I was hoping and hoping, and nothing came to pass. I did get discouraged, but faith kicked in. I constantly reminded myself that *I must have faith, joy, and happiness, despite what I am going through. I wanted to have this faith constantly. I wanted to be on faith automatic. Despite what is going on around me, I am on cruise control. I am not bothered by what happens around me.* After all, some things, you cannot do anything about but trust in the Lord. He is with you, even now.

Encourage yourself and declare God's Word over your life. Your soul will not be attacked by the spirit of fear, the spirit of anxiety, the spirit of worry, the spirit of hopelessness, or the spirit of depression. God is with you and He will take care of you!

No matter what you are going through, yes, it is going to be tough sometimes. But you need to trust God and take your eyes off the circumstances, because the more you focus on that circumstance, the worst you are going to feel. And then you will begin to operate in the flesh, making decisions in the flesh, and doing so can make matters worse. Just let it go and let God have His way. He will work it out. And even though He may not change that situation immediately, pray that He regulates your mind and gives you peace.

Read the Bible and pray every day. And I promise, if you try wholeheartedly to do this and seek the Lord, your mind will be less distracted. No longer concentrate on that circumstance, and you will have that peace, the peace that the Lord gives.

Remember, God is with us, and He is with you everywhere you go. Everything may not be perfect. You may have some hardships and suffering, but God is still with you. He was with Joseph all this time. I can imagine Joseph saying, *"Where are you, Lord?"* during his trials. Joseph triumphed to victory in the later years. So, thank God and give Him praise now. Everything the devil meant for bad, God is going to make it good.

Other readings:

- Genesis 37: 12–28
- Genesis 39–42
- Genesis 50: 20
- Proverbs 13: 12

Stay in Faith

"For we were saved in this hope, but hope that is seen is not hope; for why does one still hope for what he sees? But if we hope for what we do not see, we eagerly wait for it with perseverance." Romans 8: 24–25 (NKJV)

We must put our hope in what we do not see. This is the faith walk. Faith is the substance of things hoped for and the evidence of things unseen. Substance, faith is what holds your hope. This is why living on earth can be a challenge for the believers; the physical elements of the world, the things that you can see, can distract you from the unseen (i.e., distract you from your faith, because you don't see things turning around just yet). Sometimes, we put more credibility on what we see and hear in the physical realm, which in the end can destroy us. It can weaken our faith, and we can, therefore, lose our hope (our expectation in the things not seen yet). Faith holds your hope. Therefore, we must stay in the Word. Pray for the increase in faith. Be prepared for the challenge. Be prepared by knowing what the Word says.

Yes, this may contradict worldly views. We are so quick to focus on the natural. As believers, that's why we have what is called spiritual warfare. The Holy Spirit is tugging you one way and the flesh is pulling you another way. When you feel your natural self coming over, when you know it's not a good, peaceful feeling or suddenly you feel sad, depressed, or overwhelmed about life, begin to pray immediately and read the Word of God to encourage yourself again. Recite Romans

8: 28 (NKJV). "And we know that all things work together for good to those who love God, to those who are the called according to His purpose." Do not be overcome by the spirit of darkness. The Bible says, give no place or opportunity to the devil. Therefore, think of that ray of hope. Trust God.

When you are going through what you are going through, it does not feel great. But once you get a chance to look back over your life, you will know that it was the Lord leading you and guiding you all along. He is with you. Stay in faith!

Other readings:

- Romans 4: 19–20
- Galatians 5: 16–17
- Ephesians 4: 27

The Enemy Will Attack

"A final word: Be strong in the Lord and in his mighty power. Put on all of God's armor so that you will be able to stand firm against all strategies of the devil." Ephesians 6: 10–11 (NLT)

We must put on the whole armor of God, the shield of faith, so that we can block the fiery attacks of the enemy, whether it's your mind, emotions, physical conditions, family members, or whatever it may be. We must fight back with the sword, which is the Word of God. Fight the good fight of faith and don't give up.

We must live in expectancy. Knowing God sent His son, Jesus, to die for our sins. God forgives, and a righteous man may fall seven times, but he gets back up. When we don't get back up, this gives the enemy the opportunity to beat us and pull us down further. Don't be a victim; claim victory: You may be down, but know God is a provider, He is a healer; He changes lives and scenarios. Believe God will take care of you. He will restore the years; you must be faithful and continue to build yourself up in Christ. Remember, what you feed will grow! So, feed your spirit with God's Word and prayer, not your flesh with the customs and behaviors of this world. Romans 12: 2 (NLT) says, "Don't copy the behavior and customs of this world, but let God transform you into a new person by changing the way you think. Then you will learn to know God's will for you, which is good and pleasing and perfect."

It is the mind. The enemy will attack that because if we know no better, we will fall for what we see, feel, think, or want (now), which is feeding our flesh. That is why we must transform our mind by renewing it with God's Word, fight back against what the enemy says (say, "no"), and claim the victory! Live in peace and don't be threatened about the things of this world. We overcome the world by our faith. Trust in God and lean not to your understanding; acknowledge Him and He will guide you. You must trust God, and no matter how it seems or how you feel, have faith!

Other readings:

- Proverbs 3: 5–6
- Proverbs 24: 16
- Joel 2: 25
- 1 Timothy 6: 12
- 1 John 5: 4–5

Stand Firm

"Stay alert! Watch out for your great enemy, the devil. He prowls around like a roaring lion, looking for someone to devour. Stand firm against him, and be strong in your faith. Remember that your family of believers all over the world is going through the same kind of suffering you are. In his kindness, God called you to share in his eternal glory by means of Christ Jesus. So, after you have suffered a little while, he will restore, support, and strengthen you, and he will place you on a firm foundation. All power to him forever! Amen." 1 Peter 5: 8—11 (NLT)

The Word of God tells us that Satan (the evil one of this world) is roaring around like a hungry lion seeking, preying on the individuals he can destroy. We must remain alert and stand firm.

Look how shrewd the devil is. The devil can come through anything and anybody. He may come in as a nicely wrapped gift; he may even come through a loved one or a close friend. The devil will use anybody to get to you. So, stand firm!

Just be aware that it is the attack of the enemy (the devil/the adversary of mankind) for you to be frustrated and make you want to give up on the life, jobs, goals, and bad habits that you are trying to break. But don't; stand firm. God is a deliverer; He's a protector and a provider. He will see you through, but you must trust Him and stand firm. Give the Lord the opportunity to work things out for you. Just don't throw in the towel! One day when you look back, you will see that the Lord has been with you all along and He is with you now.

So, be careful, watchful, and alert when these things appear to happen to you. This could be the enemy attacking you in any way that he can. When this happens, you need to know the Word of God, and trust in the Lord and lean not to your own understanding. Things are not always as they appear.

Yes, it hurts when children do not obey, it hurts when people lie, it hurts when it looks like things are not coming together. It feels like you are being torn apart, but that's when you must stand firm and trust the Lord because the enemy will attack you like a lion and want to rip you apart (spiritually and emotionally). And though he may be ripping you apart through circumstances and life events, don't give up! You are kept by Jesus!

Trust God. And that's the beauty of it, because in due season, He will exalt you, and He will give you everything that you stand in need of.

Keep your mind covered with the Word of God and stay alert because the devil is looking around to see who he can destroy. It is good to know the Word of God, so you can be prepared when the enemy attacks, which he will. When he does, you will know what the Word of God says, and that is **STAND FIRM!**

Other reading:

- Proverbs 3: 5–6

Recognize the Tricks of the Enemy, the Deceiver of Mankind

"Then the serpent said to the woman, 'You will not surely die. For God knows that in the day you eat of it your eyes will be opened, and you will be like God, knowing good and evil.' So when the woman saw that the tree was good for food, that it was pleasant to the eyes, and a tree desirable to make one wise, she took of its fruit and ate. She also gave to her husband with her, and he ate." Genesis 3: 4–6 (NKJV)

No one is worth how far I have come with God. You meet a special friend who you are excited about, and the physical attraction and chemistry is there. It is like your mind becomes cloudy and you forget the Word of God (momentarily). The temptation will be there. Therefore, stay in the Word like you were in the beginning. Just because Mr. Good-looking comes along, there is no need to stop reading your Bible *daily* and praying. (This is probably when you need to read and pray more.) Satan wants to relax you, keep you occupied, and keep your mind off God. Even if this is the right relationship, God must be in the midst of it. So how do you overcome this? By meditating on the Word daily and not daydreaming about the relationship. You must replace your fleshly thoughts with godly thoughts. Read your Bible even more now. Sometimes, the enemy will see how far you have come and use it as a distraction. Keep your mind on the Father's Word. Satan tries to deceive us; he makes sin look pleasurable, as he did with Eve in the Garden of Eden.

Remember that Satan is the deceiver of all mankind. He wants us to divert our attention to elsewhere. His plan is for us to feel defeated and hopeless, not trusting in the Word of God. If you have been feeling discouraged, focus on what has been preoccupying your time and thoughts. Could these be mini distractions to keep your mind off what God has called you to do? Recognize this and hit the reset button. Have a clear mind, meditate, and pray to God. He will provide revelation to what's going on if you diligently seek Him. There is no need to lose hope; remember Joel 2:25, God will restore the years the locust took. He did it for me, and He will do it for you.

Thank God for restoring the years.

Other readings:

- Genesis 3: 1–24
- Revelation 12: 9

Trust God with the Relationship

"The Lord kept his word and did for Sarah exactly what he had promised." Genesis 21:1 (NLT)

We must be obedient to God. It will save us some heartaches.

In the Book of Genesis (Chapters 16 through 21), God told Abraham to listen to Sarah, his wife, and tell Hagar and her son (who is also Abraham's son) to leave the establishment. Can you imagine how hurt Abraham must have been to put his son and the mother of his son out? Nevertheless, Abraham was obedient to God. He put them out.

In the midst of it all, neither Abraham nor Hagar knew the plan that God had for them. God had a plan! You see, God will prompt us to do things that may seem harsh to others, or even cause us heartache, but we must let it go and let God's plan manifest in our lives.

While dating, several years ago, without a doubt, I heard God speak to me on numerous occasions. God told me that it is not him (the guy), but He (God) that I needed. The Lord told me that I needed to establish an intimate relationship with Him (God) first. However, I ignored the voice of God and that relationship brought me years of heartaches because God was not in the midst of it. As I reflect, I knew God wanted me to do something, but I could not do it with my own strength. I was living worldly and only partly godly. I became confused in this relationship. I was lukewarm in the Word of God (one foot in and one foot out). Finally, I grew tired of the mess that was that relationship. I prayed to God to show me clearly. He did. And I finally let it go and submitted myself to God. With faith, I turned away from the earthly relationship and to God. I was obedient, and God let me walk away in peace and in love.

Now, even in letting go, I had peace, but I began to experience storms of faith in my life. Circumstances arose that sometimes drained me, hurt me, and caused me to question God's promises, but now I know it was a testing of my faith. This is what happened to Sarah; she doubted God's promise for a son, so she let her servant Hagar sleep with her husband to give Abraham a son. That son was not the son God had promised. Sarah later resented Hagar and her son and told Abraham to make them leave. When we lose our faith, we mess things up. Sarah got impatient and moved ahead of God. Lean not to your own understanding. God knows all about the future and His plans for you are for the good, if you trust, believe, and remain obedient.

Other readings:

- Proverbs 3: 5
- Jeremiah 29: 11
- James 1: 3

Meditate in His Word Day and Night

"This Book of the Law shall not depart from your mouth,
but you shall meditate in it day and night, that you may
observe to do according to all that is written in it. For
then you will make your way prosperous, and then you
will have good success." Joshua 1: 8 (NKJV)

God's Word will minister to you in due time. Therefore, you must stay in the Word of God, both day and night. Read the Bible daily. Because Satan, the accuser of the brethren, will build up lies in your mind, ungodly thoughts, and fantasies.

We must meditate on God's Word for two reasons. Number one, when you meditate on God's Word day and night, you have a sense of protection, and you can be spiritually prepared for the enemy. Because if you are not standing firm on God's Word daily and don't know what the Bible says about you as a child of God and the trick of the enemy, the enemy will attack you when you are off guard. The enemy will feed you lies, and it's easier to believe a lie if you don't know the truth. In this case, you will not be prepared and will not be armored with the Word of God. You don't have the weapon to fight back, which is the Word of God. According to the power in us, we can pull down strongholds (fixated lies in our mind) that come against the knowledge (Word) of God. But if you don't know your weapon, you can't fight against the enemy.

Number two, you want to meditate on the Word day and night because life circumstances can hit hard and unexpectedly. And you will need the Word of God to encourage you and lift your spirit during such times. The Word of God can inspire you. It will give you peace. Therefore, you want to have the Word of God in your spirit always.

In the Book of Joshua, it says "meditate in it day and night." And I like to think that in between "the day and the night," anything can happen. Therefore, stay in the Word daily. In the morning, rise and shine. Thank you, Lord. Try your best to get a Word in (a scripture) and meditate on it. Think about what God's Word says. Plant the seed of faith in your heart, so throughout the day, you can have something to fall back on. And then, when you go to bed at night, you want to thank God and meditate on the Word as you go to sleep. The Word will resonate in your spirit while sleeping. You will wake up refreshed for the new day ahead.

Stay in the Word of God both day and night. You must.

Other readings:

- 2 Corinthians 10: 4–5
- Revelation 12: 10

Strongholds

"For though we walk in the flesh, we do not war according to the flesh. For the weapons of our warfare are not carnal but mighty in God for pulling down strongholds, casting down arguments and every high thing that exalts itself against the knowledge of God, bringing every thought into captivity to the obedience of Christ." 2 Corinthians 10: 3–5 (NKJV)

Though we walk in the flesh, we do not war according to the flesh. We wage war in the spirit, not in the flesh. Recognize what or who you are fighting against! The Greek word for stronghold is a fortress. You have authority to pull down strongholds. The stronghold is in the human mind. It is a fortified place where negative thoughts are trapped or collected, fortified in your mind. The enemy considered this a permanent place of his dwelling to keep you bound and afraid, but I declare no. According to the Word of God, we have weapons that are mighty in God for pulling down strongholds and casting down every false thought. Those spiritual weapons are the Word of God, faith, and prayer.

Some strongholds built in our minds keep us from stepping out in faith. We stay in that safety zone far too long, because of fear. We listen to those lies, such as *I can't, what if this happens, what will they think of me,* or *what if they found out this or that.* Those thoughts, if they come against the Word of God, are all lies to keep you in the same place of fear of the unknown.

These strongholds in your mind are the places of the enemy's entrance. They keep you bound in negative wrong thinking and doing. In the name of Jesus, we have the authority to cast down strongholds and every other high thing that exalts itself against the Word of God. If you have been born again, you have a Redeemer. He defeated the enemy years ago on Calvary. Because you have been redeemed by the blood of Jesus and righteous living, you now must resist the devil and all evil forces that come against you. You see, you must find those scriptures that speak about life and go against those false thoughts. Find scripture and hold on to it to erase those thoughts. This battle is spiritual. Our weapons are mighty in God. Pray always, have faith, show love, and keep hope in all things. Line your thoughts up with the Word of God and meditate on what is good. Tell the enemy you don't believe his lies, in the name of Jesus, and cite scriptures.

Other reading:

- Ephesians 1: 17–23

Keep the Perspective

"For as he thinketh in his heart, so is he." Proverbs 23: 7 (KJV)

Today is the day to reflect. Don't lose your perspective of things. Think great thoughts. You attract what you think. Move forward, knowing great things are happening in your life right now. You just don't see it in the natural realm, but it's happening! You also must believe it and accept in your spirit that great results are coming your way.

Repeat to yourself the great things you want. For example, say, "I have confidence and I am not shaken by what I feel or see now!" Trust God and lean not to your own understanding. Acknowledge God and He will guide you.

Trust me, I have been there with mind-boggling thoughts. Change your thoughts, change your life. The Bible says, what a man thinks in his heart, is he so. From out of the heart flows the issues of life, so guard your heart. Have a super-rich, faithful day.

Other readings:

- Proverbs 3: 5
- Proverbs 4: 23
- Proverbs 23: 7

Living Single

*"Trust in the L*ORD *with all your heart, and lean not on your*
own understanding; in all your ways acknowledge Him, and
He shall direct your paths." Proverbs 3: 5–6 (NKJV)

Single and having peace of mind. For the Word of God says that your
Creator will be your husband. Keep God first. Take hold of the scriptures, and when you do that's when your earthly spouse will come.
The Word of God is true. However, you must do your part. Develop a
close intimate relationship with Him first and then all else will fall in
place, according to His will for your life. The Lord will not withhold
any good thing from those who do what is right. Obedience is better
than sacrifice.

I recall being a single woman, and I remember those moments. I
did not have peace of mind. It seemed as if something was missing. I
was tainted by the ways of the world, and the Lord had to prune me.
I learned later that we, as believers, can't expect to receive anything
from God when we stand divided between the flesh (what you want)
and the spirit (what God calls you to do).

God can fill any void you may have, so don't run around trying
to fill it yourself. Stay busy in your work for the Lord, and it will work

out simply fine! You will see.

Other readings:

- 1 Samuel 15: 22
- Psalm 84: 11
- Isaiah 54: 5
- James 1: 6

Free Within: Serenity

"Do not be anxious or worried about anything, but in everything [every circumstance and situation] by prayer and petition with thanksgiving, continue to make your [specific] requests known to God. And the peace of God [that peace which reassures the heart, that peace] which transcends all understanding, [that peace which] stands guard over your hearts and your minds in Christ Jesus [is yours]." Philippians 4 : 6–7 (AMP)

This is a good day. Many things we complain about or are troubled about are outside of us (i.e., worldly matters and conditions). So how does one learn to have the serenity within during these troubled times; that is, how can one find calmness or peace? I believe we need to know that God is not the author of confusion. He is the God of peace. We need to be steadfast and strong in our faith. The Lord Jesus Christ gives rest to all who are weary and to those who carry heavy burdens. You will find rest for your souls in Christ Jesus. Go to Him and find your peace.

Other readings:

- Matthew 11 : 28–30
- 1 Corinthians 14 : 33

Enlarge Your Faith—I Will Not Be Destroyed

"You intended to harm me, but God intended it all for good. He brought me to this position so I could save the lives of many people." Genesis 50: 20 (NLT)

You must have continuous faith and strength. You can't keep crying and complaining about what people have done to you or what has happened to you. Don't you know that all this causes anxiety? By replaying your worst thoughts, you are creating the distress. Satan is using the situation as bait to attack your faith. But God will turn this situation around for your good. Keep your mind on what is good. The Word of God says, we must endure suffering during the times of trouble. Be patient and pray always. The Bible teaches us about suffering, but the Bible continuously encourages believers to have trust, hope, endurance, and patience. Enlarge your faith. You will not be destroyed. Trust in the Lord.

Other readings:

- Isaiah 54: 1–17
- Romans 12: 12

Misery Loves Company

"Don't worry about the wicked or envy those who do wrong. For like grass, they soon fade away. Like spring flowers, they soon wither. Trust in the LORD and do good. Then you will live safely in the land and prosper. Take delight in the LORD, and he will give you your heart's desires. Commit everything you do to the LORD. Trust him, and he will help you. He will make your innocence radiate like the dawn, and the justice of your cause will shine like the noonday sun." Psalm 37: 1–6 (NLT)

Misery loves company in so many ways.

Relationships. You decided to end the relationship. The damage has been done. Move on, and don't let uncontrollable bad thoughts hold you back from pursuing what must be. This is one reason why you were in the unhealthy relationship for so long: fear and doubt. You will be fine. Trust in the Lord.

Trials and tribulations. Trials are going to come. The mature recognize that trials will come. Take time to pray your way through them. People will upset you during the day. The day will not always be the way you want. You can't say everything you want to say, because Satan will use that against you.

Learn to endure and be patient. Wait on the Lord, and He will renew your strength. He will give you strength for today and tomorrow. You are not alone.

Other reading:

- Isaiah 40: 31

A Clear Conscience

"Everything is pure to those whose hearts are pure. But nothing is pure to those who are corrupt and unbelieving, because their minds and consciences are corrupted. Such people claim they know God, but they deny him by the way they live. They are detestable and disobedient, worthless for doing anything good." Titus 1: 15–16 (NLT)

Because of your customary way of doing things and thinking things (particularly the ways of the world), your conscience is weakening. A weak conscience is easily violated. Conscience is influenced by your surroundings. To be full of love and to do the work of the Lord, you must have a pure, healthy, clear conscience, and genuine faith. A clear conscience does not have preconceived ideas or judgments of a person or a situation.

Other reading:

- 1 Corinthians 6: 12

Temptation

"No temptation [regardless of its source] has overtaken or enticed you that is not common to human experience [nor is any temptation unusual or beyond human resistance]; but God is faithful [to His word—He is compassionate and trustworthy], and He will not let you be tempted beyond your ability [to resist], but along with the temptation He [has in the past and is now and] will [always] provide the way out as well, so that you will be able to endure it [without yielding, and will overcome temptation with joy]. Therefore, my beloved, run [keep far, far away] from [any sort of] idolatry [and that includes loving anything more than God, or participating in anything that leads to sin and enslaves the soul]." 1 Corinthians 10: 13–14 (AMP)

Temptation happens to everyone. However, remember, God will not put more on you than you can bear. And there is always an escape for you if you really want it.

We must learn from our mistakes, and one way to do that is to keep studying the Bible regularly. Recognize people and environments that will entice you and turn away from them. Particularly, turn away from those things that you know are wrong and will lead down the wrong path. Pray to do what is right and find new friends who preferably know God and can help you stay on the right track.

Remember, Satan is the one who tempts us with an idea or thought. He tries to contradict the Word of God. But we have a choice: to yield or not to yield. Therefore, know the Word of God and stand on His Word, despite what it feels like, looks like, or sounds like. Yield that flesh.

Other readings:

- Genesis 3: 1–4
- Psalm 1: 1

Generations Need to Be Taught

*"After that generation died, another generation grew up who
did not acknowledge the Lord or remember the mighty things
he had done for Israel. The Israelites did evil in the Lord's sight
and served the images of Baal." Judges 2:10–11 (NLT)*

We must wake up. Do you see all the evil that's going on in this world?
Little by little, it gets worse and worse, more corrupt behavior. It's
evident that sin stunts spiritual growth. Next thing you know, we don't
pray as much or as long as we used to, we skip Bible study, we get angry
easily. What's going on here? It's time to turn back.

The Bible is a road map. History does repeat itself. The Book of
Judges was written more than two thousand years ago, and it still holds
true today.

It seems that generation after generation loses sight of God. Maybe
it's because great-grandmothers and great-grandfathers and God-fear-
ing aunts and uncles are gone on to glory, and the Word of God is not
being instilled in our younger generation as it once was. Perhaps the
age at which girls become pregnant has an impact. A firm relationship with God may not be as strong for young-aged parents due to so
many other worldly distractions that make it even harder for the young
mother or father to instill truths in their child. Or could it be that children have not been raised in a faith-type environment, but they have
witnessed the goodness of the Lord. And so, when they become older,

they really don't know God for themselves and somehow the faith in the family-line has been lost. This is what the Bible says in Judges 2:10 (NLT): "After that generation died, another generation grew up who did not acknowledge the Lord or remember the mighty things he had done for Israel." It's a cycle; we need to wake up.

In the Book of Joshua, Joshua led the people to the Promised Land. The Lord had a covenant with Israel, and He will not break His covenant. The Lord had sworn this back in the Book of Genesis to Joseph and Moses, the forefathers. However, the new generation entered the Promised Land and did not do what the Lord told them to do. He told them to drive out the inhabitants and they did not, and they lived among them; therefore, it became a thorn in their back.

This is how life is. God tells us to do something or place a promise in our hearts, and when that promise comes to pass, we don't do our parts. We don't keep our promises to God. As a result, there are consequences. And those consequences can be a thorn for us. Learn from this Book of Life, the Bible.

Other readings:

- Joshua 21: 43–45
- Judges 2: 1–3
- Proverbs 22: 6

Living at Peace with Others

"If possible, as far as it depends on you, live at peace with everyone." Romans 12: 18 (AMP)

Live at peace with God, others, and yourself. If you are not at peace with what you're doing or saying, don't do it. It is the best practice to follow. It's that simple.

Other reading:

- Matthew 22: 37–39

Worry and Seeking the Kingdom

"And some fell among thorns, and the thorns grew up, and choked it, and it yielded no fruit." Mark 4: 7 (KJV)

In Matthew 6: 25–34, Jesus teaches us not to worry. Why? Because if we are not careful, the cares of this world will choke the Word out of us. The cares and concerns of this world are the things of the flesh (e.g., relationships, peer pressure, job, finances, situations that develop). Even though you have faith...be watchful.

The parable of the sower in Mark, Chapter 4 tells us that we have the Word of God in us, but we let the cares of this world choke the Word out of us. And we have so little faith. Have you ever experienced being high on the Lord, full of praise, and then something—the cares of the world—come and knock you down? The key is getting back up.

It's so amazing when I know that I have faith and a relationship with God, plus I am assured that everything is going to be alright; I can still find myself in doubt, crying, and concerned. At one point, I tried to analyze why this is. *Is it because I don't know what tomorrow is going to hold, or is it that my current situation has gotten the best of me?* Whatever it is or was—as in the Book of Job—I did not have the answer, but I learned to let go and give it to God. So, I stopped worrying about things as much as I could and prayed for release of such carnal (worldly) thoughts. I did not let the cares of this world dominate my thinking, because the Word of God says these things dominate the thoughts of unbelievers, and my Heavenly Father already knows what I need. And I know that I am a believer.

The Book of Matthew says worrying does not add a single moment to your life. And as I look back over my life, when I worried, it added nothing but stress, headaches, and ulcers.

Just give it to God! Whatever you are worrying about, give it to God, and then you won't constantly have that stuff on your mind! Clear your mind. You cannot do anything when you are worried. You will either sleep, become lazy, drink, eat, or shop. All of which can be detrimental, if done too excessively.

The Bible tells us to cast our cares to God, and He will give us rest. We will have peaceful minds. Wake up each morning refreshed. It's a great day. Live each day intentionally. Everything does not have to be a rush, because that's how the enemy chokes the Word out of you. You are just too busy to stay in the Word, so you have no armor to prepare yourself for what lies ahead.

Do you see that there must be a balance? I have learned that for as much as I am in the world, I must have an equal or double dose of God's Word. The world is becoming more open, and it's easy to fall prey to Satan's tricks.

Stay in the Word and you will have peace, I guarantee you! Seek the kingdom first and live righteously, and all things will be added. As all things will be added, you should not worry. But you must do your part first. The scriptures say first seek the kingdom and second live righteously, and then the promise is that all things will be added. God will give you what you stand in need of. It works, but it may not work overnight. God molds us into what He wants us to be, so He can use us for His purpose. Amen.

Other readings:

- Proverbs 24: 16
- Mark 4: 1–20
- Matthew 6: 33

Keep Close

"Therefore I tell you, stop being worried or anxious (perpetually uneasy, distracted) about your life, as to what you will eat or what you will drink; nor about your body, as to what you will wear. Is life not more than food, and the body more than clothing? Look at the birds of the air; they neither sow [seed] nor reap [the harvest] nor gather [the crops] into barns, and yet your heavenly Father keeps feeding them. Are you not worth much more than they?" Matthew 6: 25–26 (AMP)

Don't allow Satan and the ways of the world distract you from the things of God. Otherwise, you feel hopeless; you will move further away from the ray of hope. You must stay in the Word daily. Meditate on it both day and night. That's the only way you will succeed.

Encourage yourself in the Lord, even if you don't feel like it. Turn on your favorite gospel music, praise song, or read a scripture, and, before you know it, you have joy in your spirit. Your perspective changes. Your mind is off the situation. That's the difference between being in the darkness (i.e., spiritual darkness) and having the light in your life. The darkness keeps you down, but Jesus is the light of the world. The Lord is near to all who calls Him and He watches over those He loves. He watches over you, despite what you see or how you feel. Reconcile yourself back to God. Restore your mind with the things of

God now that you have clarity and see the trick of the enemy.

Other readings:

- Joshua 1: 8
- Psalm 145: 18

Don't Throw Away This Great Confident Trust

"So do not throw away this confident trust in the Lord. Remember the great reward it brings you! Patient endurance is what you need now, so that you will continue to do God's will. Then you will receive all that he has promised." Hebrews 10: 35–36 (NLT)

Do not throw away this great confident trust in the Lord; God can be trusted to keep His promises. We must have patience and endurance right now. That's what we need in a time like this, so that we can continue to carry out God's will. Once we do this, we will then see His promises fulfilled. We must stay reminded that God is not like man; He doesn't lie. God keeps His promises.

We can trust God. For all that I have been through over these years learning and growing in God's Word, this is a great scripture because I know that I can't throw away this great confidence. The hope I know that I have to trust in God. And there will be times when you may grow weary. And when this happens, redirect your focus; you can't lose your focus. You must focus on the Lord. Over the past years, I always tell myself that I am a woman of faith, not a woman of doubt (three times). Encourage yourself and have faith.

Faith is the substance of things hoped for and the evidence of things unseen. That's why in the flesh (your natural self), you will see things. In the flesh, you will hear things; those things will come to shake your faith. Faith is not in what you see or hear. It's the evidence of things unseen. So, we can't get caught up in the things that we see and the things that we hear. We must have faith, and with faith comes the Holy Spirit. Let the Holy Spirit guide your life. Then you will not grow weary, because you know God and God can be trusted.

Scripture tells us that the flesh and the spirit are always wrestling. Romans Chapter 8 says the Lord sent Jesus to die for our sins, and because Jesus died for our sins, sin does not control us anymore. We have no obligation to do what the sinful nature (the flesh) wants, because now we have the Spirit of God, the Holy Spirit.

Yes, walking in the spirit can be a challenge (it is a narrow path), but the Bible says a life following the Spirit leads to life and peace. The Word of God says He comes to give us life more abundantly and peace. Do you want a life of peace? We can be in this world and not live, figuratively speaking. Make the decision. Focus on God and let the Holy Spirit guide your life. It will help you make the right decisions, and you will live a life of peace no matter what's going on.

What is peace? Peace is not that all your bills are paid and everything is going well—that's not peace. Peace is when your bills are not paid, when you're facing family crisis, when things seem to be falling apart, but, during the storm, you can still have peace. God can give you peace when things are not going well in the world, so you have peace of mind and heart.

So, don't throw away this great confidence. You must trust in God and let the Holy Spirit guide your mind. The fruit of the spirit is love, joy, peace, long-suffering, kindness, gentleness, goodness, faithfulness, and self-control.

Other readings:

- Romans 8: 1–17
- Galatians 5: 22–23

You Are Not Crazy; The Devil Just Wants to Take You Out

"As Jesus was climbing out of the boat, a man who was possessed by demons came out to meet him. For a long time he had been homeless and naked, living in the tombs outside the town." Luke 8: 27 (NLT)

God places people in our lives to help them, not to judge them. Spirits are real. Demonic forces are real. The Word of God is real!

There is a passage in the Gospel of Luke that speaks of how we can come to God for deliverance, and then we turn back and go out there and do the same thing again, after knowing what the Word of God says. The evil spirit and the demonic forces come back even greater. You made a good attempt to get cleaned up, but you did not consistently fill that empty space, your inner man, with the Word of God. So, the same spirit returns with more strength.

Certain evil spirits feed on other types of evil spirits. Satan will have you thinking you are crazy. And it is so true about the environments you are in; you keep going out there and sinning. Particularly when you know what the Word of God says, it will come on you so great that you will think you are crazy. This is scripture-based. In the Gospel of Luke, the man was running around with his clothes off, as if he was crazy. But those were the satanic forces upon him. He was filled with legions of evil spirits (many). Jesus delivered him and the man was fully clothed and in his right mind.

Know the devil comes to steal, kill, and destroy. He wants to take you out. He puts suicidal thoughts in your mind, making you think you are crazy—particularly when you are strong enough and have been delivered—knowing that you will have a great testimony.

The Word of God is true! The healer is the Word of God. The comforter is the Word of God. We must fight off those temptations. If you keep going out there doing the same thing, those evil spirits are going to attack you more in your mind. *You know, it's the flesh and the spirit waging war against one another.*

My prayer: "Lord, I pray for peace and Satan gets his hand off your people who are seeking your face but keep getting tangled in the world. I pray that your people stay away from environments that eat them up [harmful, toxic]. Remove any kind of addictions in this world that keeps people from coming to know your will for their life. Lord, deliver them and set them free; show them the way and give them strength. In Jesus' name, Amen."

Other readings:

- Luke 11: 24–26
- 2 Peter 2: 20–22

No Condemnation

*"But He was wounded for our transgressions, He was bruised
for our iniquities; the chastisement for our peace was upon Him,
and by His stripes we are healed."* Isaiah 53: 5 (NKJV)

Even though we are in Christ and believers, as we journey through
life reaching that higher calling, our flesh or the devil can cause us to
think about past sins and mistakes, and make us feel bad (condemnation). But remember what is written in the Book of Isaiah, Jesus was
wounded for our transgressions, bruised for our iniquities, the chastisement for our peace was upon Him, and by His stripes we are healed.
Do not believe the lies of the enemy. Jesus paid the ultimate price for
sinners. This is why we need to plead the blood of Jesus over our lives.
He died on Calvary for our sins; He was bruised for our iniquities—
the price has been paid, so stop letting the devil condemn you. There
is no condemnation for he that is in Christ.

Thank you, Lord, for the blood of the Lamb. And, as we come to
know this more, we will be at peace. We can walk in liberty knowing
God gave us a new life. Yes, we can start all over. We can walk in peace
and walk in faith, trusting and believing, casting our cares upon the
Lord. The Lord is faithful and just!

Author's Note: You must be careful about this. This is an old trick of the enemy to condemn you and make you feel bad and lost again. Satan wants you to give up and revert to your old self and negative thinking. Keep the shield of faith and your thoughts on what is good!

Other reading:

- Romans 8: 1–11

Morning by Morning, New Mercies I See

"Through the LORD's mercies we are not consumed, because His compassions fail not. They are new every morning; great is Your faithfulness. 'The LORD is my portion', says my soul, 'Therefore I hope in Him!' The LORD is good to those who wait for Him, to the soul who seeks Him." Lamentations 3: 22–25 (NKJV)

Encourage yourself: You must know, without any ounce of doubt, that God is working things out. Do you recall the feeling of knowing that God is going to work it out? I encourage you to believe and trust in that! Just close your eyes and imagine that good thought: *God will take care of me.* Smile and go in peace.

Other reading:

- Numbers 6: 24–26

Stress and Body: Don't Worry, Be Happy

"Finally, brethren, whatever things are true, whatever things are noble, whatever things are just, whatever things are pure, whatever things are lovely, whatever things are of good report, if there is any virtue and if there is anything praiseworthy— meditate on these things. The things which you learned and received and heard and saw in me, these do, and the God of peace will be with you." Philippians 4: 8–9 (NKJV)

Troubled in your mind? Feeling a bit stressed? Sometimes, we must stop and ask ourselves what is causing the anxiety. Could it be your own way of thinking that is driving the worries and stress? I told myself as I am telling you, "You just have to be content, regardless." Learn to be content whether things are going well or not so well. Read the Word and be grateful for everything because that will change you. You must make yourself happy. This means don't let your happiness be predicated on happenings (people, places, and things).

Stay in the Word of God and when circumstances come, which they will, start reading the Word. Stay focused on the Word of God. Because otherwise, once you begin to meditate (think hard) on that negative stuff, it will wear on you and drain you. Stress kills. It will mess up both the inside and the outside of you.

The Word of God tells us that it is best to fill our minds up and meditate on things that are true, noble, and honorable, not things that are the worst, bad, and non-praiseworthy. We must keep this in mind: Meditate on the goodness.

So that's what we must do. We must have joy, despite what we feel. It is a great feeling, and it is healthy for your body. A merry heart is like good medicine for the soul! We do worry, and we will have trouble from time to time, but we must turn that over to the Lord! Amen.

Other readings:

- Proverbs 17: 22
- Philippians 4: 11–12

We Must Do the Work While We Can

*"Jesus answered, 'Neither this man nor his parents sinned,
but that the works of God should be revealed in him. I must
work the works of Him who sent Me while it is day; the night
is coming when no one can work. As long as I am in the world,
I am the light of the world.'"John 9: 3–5 (NKJV)*

Jesus was talking with His disciples, and they came across a blind man.
The man was born blind, and the disciples asked Jesus was it the result
of his sin or his parents' sin. Jesus said, "No." And then Jesus said, "I am
the light of the world, and I must go out and do the works of He who
sent me." Jesus healed the blind man by putting mud on his eyes. And
the blind man went out to the world showing everyone, and people
could not believe it. For those who believed, they knew Jesus was the
Messiah. Miracles and testimonies that people can show the work of
the Lord. Jesus healed the man, and the man went out to the world, and
this is one way to communicate about this man called Jesus.

The irony in this biblical story is that Jesus said He is the light of
the world. The man was blind and couldn't see; he was in darkness.
Jesus healed the man's eyes and now he can see the light. In this world,
people are spiritually blind and can't see and, as a result, live in darkness, not realizing Jesus is the light.

Have you been procrastinating on certain tasks God has laid on your heart? Procrastination is a thief. You don't want to get caught up in years of sitting and not doing what God has sent you to do. It's time to make a move. The Word says, "I must work the works of Him who sent Me, while it is day; the night is coming when no one can work." (John 9: 4 NKJV)

What is your purpose? You can't fulfill it if you are harboring any guilt, shame, anger, or plain old slothfulness. You must be careful, because the enemy is roaring around like a lion to see who he can distract from doing good. He wants to keep us from doing good work through negative self-talk and destroying relationships. The Word of God says we come to help people. We can't help them if we are not displaying the fruit of the spirit: love, joy, peace, long-suffering, kindness, goodness, faithfulness, gentleness, and self-control.

We must demonstrate the work of He who sent us, and there will be distractions along the way. Remember, Jesus is the light of the world, and we are His disciples. We must demonstrate the power of God through our testimonies that will help and heal people. Jesus is the light and if He is in us, we have the light to shine in dark places. Let your light shine!

Other readings:

- Galatians 5: 22–23
- Revelation 12: 11

Night Will Come When No One Can Work—Stay Positive and Carry On

"Now as Jesus passed by, He saw a man who was blind from birth. And His disciples asked Him, saying, 'Rabbi, who sinned, this man or his parents, that he was born blind?' Jesus answered, 'Neither this man nor his parents sinned, but that the works of God should be revealed in him. I must work the works of Him who sent Me while it is day; the night is coming when no one can work. As long as I am in the world, I am the light of the world.'" John 9: 1–5 (NKJV)

Sometimes, we have seasons in our life that we don't understand. During the tough season in your life, keep your head up high and walk through it. It is during those seasons when we keep the faith and don't throw in the towel that we see the demonstration of God's power.

Things will happen in our lives that seem unfair and we don't have the answer to the why. But remember, God gets good out of evil and all things work out for the good to those who believe and belong to God.

We must have faith. Faith is the substance of things hoped for and the evidence of things unseen. Believe it will actually happen, even though you don't see it. This is a testimony: walk through the storms of life. People are saved through others' testimonies.

We must be busy with God's business. Don't be distracted by stuff that means nothing, and don't be discouraged. We all must try to do the work of He who sent us. The night will come when no one can work. There is a beginning and an end to all things.

Other readings:

- Genesis 50: 20
- Ecclesiastes 3: 1–8
- Romans 8: 28
- Hebrews 11: 1

Don't Straddle the Fence

*"I don't mean to say that I have already achieved these things
or that I have already reached perfection. But I press on to
possess that perfection for which Christ Jesus first possessed
me. No, dear brothers and sisters, I have not achieved it, but I
focus on this one thing: Forgetting the past and looking forward
to what lies ahead, I press on to reach the end of the race and
receive the heavenly prize for which God, through Christ
Jesus, is calling us. Let all who are spiritually mature agree
on these things. If you disagree on some point, I believe God
will make it plain to you. But we must hold on to the progress
we have already made." Philippians 3: 12–16 (NLT)*

When you are going through your faith journey, there will be times
when you want to go back, but in the Book of Isaiah, it tells us to not
remember the former things nor consider the things of the old. God
is about to do a new thing.

We must trust in God and let Him do this new thing in our life.
First, we can't dip into the world. Be careful of what we listen to. Even
certain secular music will make you feel things or may make you want
to do certain things of the world that do not line up with the Word of
God or God's will for your life. Second, we must be mindful of our own

negative thoughts and lean not to our understanding. You may have to set up boundaries and rules for yourself. Even people from your past may call or text you—for what? If they have hurt you, you ended that relationship or friendship for a reason. Don't go backward, spring forward. Stay focused. Trust God.

Don't straddle the fence: stay on track!

Other readings:

- Proverbs 3: 5
- Isaiah 43: 18–19

The Flesh Will Manipulate You

*"When you follow the desires of your sinful nature, the results
are very clear: sexual immorality, impurity, lustful pleasures,
idolatry, sorcery, hostility, quarreling, jealousy, outbursts of
anger, selfish ambition, dissension, division, envy, drunkenness,
wild parties, and other sins like these. Let me tell you again,
as I have before, that anyone living that sort of life will not
inherit the Kingdom of God." Galatians 5: 19–21 (NLT)*

This is about your flesh. The flesh, yes, your own flesh will manipulate you. Your flesh can have you think certain things that are absurd or have you to believe something that is not. So you must be careful and ask yourself: "Does this line up with the Word of God? Why am I thinking about this? Has God spoken to me about this?"

As you try your best to walk on the path of faith and trusting in God, your flesh will, eventually, begin to yearn for something that you have not had in a long time or lust for something that you want badly. It will have you believe or think that every opportunity that comes to pass is for you! Because the flesh is the flesh, it will deceive you. Your flesh has been entangled in this world since birth and may perhaps be conformed to the ways of the world. So, you must be careful.

I recall when situations presented themselves to me and I thought they were for me: my opportunities. And when I look back, I think,

Wow, I can't believe I was thinking like that. So, you must be on guard, because the flesh will manipulate you and have you thinking certain things. It is unexplainable how it is when you are in it. You don't really see it, you know. You can be caught up and blinded by your emotions—the way you feel—your wants and desires for the now.

We must learn how to turn away from the flesh. You must, because the flesh will manipulate you, deceive you, and keep you from God's will for your life. And you don't want to be wandering like the Israelites in the Book of Exodus. They were responding to their flesh; they began to think about how it used to be in Egypt. They were complaining and, as a result, they wandered for some time. And that is how life can be: wandering in the same spot, in the same situation, and dealing with the same circumstances.

I can think back to when I was in those spots in my life; I remember being in them, but I did not know how to get out of them. As I look back, I ask myself why I didn't just wake up (ding-dong) and get out of it, but it's not that easy. And sometimes, if you are not mature in the spirit or constant in the Word of God, it will not be easy. And unfortunately, sometimes, it is the suffering that gets our attention. It is the suffering that draws us closer to God. When you begin to seriously pray and seek God for yourself, you will find Him and get to know Him for yourself. The Word of God says the prayer of the righteous is very powerful, and those prayers were powerful. Thank you, Lord, for your saving grace. Crucify the flesh, so it will not manipulate you.

Other readings:

- Psalm 119: 71
- Romans 12: 2
- Ephesians 2: 10
- James 5: 16

Selection of a Mate

"Seek the Kingdom of God above all else, and live righteously, and he will give you everything you need." Matthew 6: 33 (NLT)

This scripture resonates with me. Sometime ago, I remember saying, "I am going to seek the Kingdom." As I reflect, it's amazing how I sought the Kingdom, but I did not do so fully. I prayed and trusted God for everything else, but when I got into a relationship, I did not trust Him. I took matters into my own hands and the results were failure, until I wholeheartedly sought the Kingdom of God first.

To the young, unwed ladies, yes, it may be a challenge but consider this: If you trust God in all other areas in your life, why not in the selection of a mate? Do this, and your obedience will save you from heartaches. I now realize the reason why I did not trust God with the relationship: It was the flesh and my conformity to the ways of the world. Early on, I knew no better, but later I learned to do what is right. As women, we must realize that we must have self-control because the flesh (i.e., the feelings and emotions within) can be very powerful. Therefore, we need to turn over any relationship concern to God and let Him choose our mate, who is God's best. Seek the Kingdom first, and all other things will fall into place according to His will for your life. And whatever it may be, you will be blessed and happy, because now your thoughts are in alignment with God and His Word.

Other reading:

- Isaiah 54: 5

Comparing Life to Israel

"What does all this mean? Even though the Gentiles were not trying to follow God's standards, they were made right with God. And it was by faith that this took place. But the people of Israel, who tried so hard to get right with God by keeping the law, never succeeded. Why not? Because they were trying to get right with God by keeping the law instead of by trusting in him. They stumbled over the great rock in their path. God warned them of this in the Scriptures when he said, 'I am placing a stone in Jerusalem that makes people stumble, a rock that makes them fall. But anyone who trusts in him will never be disgraced.'" Romans 9: 30–33 (NLT)

The Israelites failed because they tried to get right with God by keeping the law instead of trusting God. The Gentiles, who were not trying to follow the law, were made right with God. It was by faith that that took place, and that's what we must do today! Faith and trusting God go hand in hand. Because trusting God requires faith, and having faith means trusting God.

As I think about my life, I can parallel my faith journey with the Israelites. During such a period of my life, I was just wandering. I remember a longtime friend and co-worker telling me, "You are being like the Israelites, wandering in the wilderness, going across the same mountain over and over again." At that point of my life, that was true. But then! I remember coming to the point of elevation from the wilderness. The next level was making a move to the Promised Land (i.e., the place God promised me). On my way to the Promised Land, it was not easy and I soon realized this and got tired of Satan beating me up, abusing me, and oppressing me. So, I took another step of faith forward. Along the way, came another level: complaining. There were some hurdles, and there was a point when I was so close to the Promised Land that I wanted to turn back. I began to think about the old ways, just being complacent and wanting to return, because that was my safety zone.

You see, like the scripture teaches us, there will be stages in our life (both comfortable and uncomfortable) as we journey to the Promised Land (wherever that place may be for you). But we must trust God and He will direct our path. We cannot get there in our own strength, or just by keeping the law (scripture). We must have faith and trust God. You see, I repeatedly tried to live right by obeying the scripture—to do good—but had little to no faith. When issues surfaced, I had some form of doubt.

One time, I sold my house; I stepped out on faith and decided to sell it for sale by owner. God taught me to trust Him. I had no real estate agent, and I sold my house in less than ninety days with no real estate agent. Additionally, I was approved a job transfer and was able to relocate to another state. I trusted God and not in the works of myself or others. No matter what things look like, trust God.

Other readings:

- Proverbs 3: 5–6
- Mark 11: 22

Faith

_"Then the L_ORD _said to Elijah, 'Go and live in the village of Zarephath, near the city of Sidon. I have instructed a widow there to feed you.' So he went to Zarephath. As he arrived at the gates of the village, he saw a widow gathering sticks, and he asked her, 'Would you please bring me a little water in a cup?' As she was going to get it, he called to her, 'Bring me a bite of bread, too.' But she said, 'I swear by the L_ORD _your God that I don't have a single piece of bread in the house. And I have only a handful of flour left in the jar and a little cooking oil in the bottom of the jug. I was just gathering a few sticks to cook this last meal, and then my son and I will die.' But Elijah said to her, 'Don't be afraid! Go ahead and do just what you've said, but make a little bread for me first. Then use what's left to prepare a meal for yourself and your son. For this is what the L_ORD_, the God of Israel, says: There will always be flour and olive oil left in your containers until the time when the L_ORD _sends rain and the crops grow again!' So she did as Elijah said, and she and Elijah and her family continued to eat for many days. There was always enough flour and olive oil left in the containers, just as the L_ORD _had promised through Elijah." 1 Kings 17: 8–16 (NLT)_

Faith can change anyone. You must have faith, and faith comes by hearing and reading the Word of God. This passage talks about Elijah and a widow. This is a story of faith, and when I think to myself, I thank God because when I sincerely seek Him, He always has a comforting Word for me.

This text blessed me one morning. Despite what I saw or felt in the natural, I realized I must trust God. I was led to this text in the Bible based on my given circumstance. (As I have said for every situation in life, the answer can be found in the Bible.)

Here goes the text: Despite what the widow saw in the physical realm (a little bit of flour), in the end, based on her act of faith and trusting in the Lord's promise, she always had enough leftovers. Elijah commanded the widow to make him a small cake and some for herself and her son. I am sure the widow thought, *"How can I do all this with what little I have?"* Even before Elijah told her to make the small cake, she had already settled in her mind that she only had a handful of flour and a little oil, enough to prepare for her and her son to eat and die. This widow thought this was it! But, Elijah, a man of God, had a different perspective. On the other hand, he said, "Go make me a small cake and afterwards make some for yourself and son." Did you notice the phrase "and make some afterwards for yourself and son"? This makes it sound like she had additional or, better yet, Elijah spoke of abundance (he spoke with faith).

You just can't go by what you see; you must have faith and act upon it. Say this with me, "Despite what I see, I am a (wo)man of faith. I know God's promises over my life."

And there is another side of faith in this biblical story. God spoke to Elijah and told him that He had a widow there that was going to provide. So, Elijah had to go by what the Lord told him and follow the Lord's instructions. Faith also comes with following the Lord's instructions, because once you get going and obey the Lord, He will order your steps and everything will fall into place. Amen.

Other readings:

- Psalm 119: 133
- Romans 10: 17

We Have Our Own Egypt and Promised Land Experiences

"Now go and call together all the elders of Israel. Tell them, 'Yahweh, the God of your ancestors—the God of Abraham, Isaac, and Jacob—has appeared to me. He told me, 'I have been watching closely, and I see how the Egyptians are treating you. I have promised to rescue you from your oppression in Egypt. I will lead you to a land flowing with milk and honey— the land where the Canaanites, Hittites, Amorites, Perizzites, Hivites, and Jebusites now live.'" Exodus 3:16-17 (NLT)

We all, at different points of our lives, may have had our Egypt or Promised Land experience; you may have experienced a moment of hardship and oppression or joy, praise, and abundance. Also, we may have found ourselves in the wilderness, wandering in cycles.

Think for a moment: Have you had your Egypt experience, that place of oppression, defeat, challenges, hopelessness, and darkness? We know there is a Promised Land! God is trying to get us there. We must trust in God. We believe in God, but we are not where we need to be wholeheartedly. Sometimes, while trying to get there, we fall. The Bible says a righteous man falls seven times, but he gets back up. We are trying to do the right thing. We fall every now and then. Before we know it, we have wandered for a certain time span. We have wandered in the same place and have gotten nowhere, so now we feel defeated. But there is hope.

We are out of Egypt; we are out of that place and on our way to the Promised Land, the land of abundance, "flowing with milk and honey" (figuratively speaking). Slowly but surely, we began to miss Egypt, because getting to the Promised Land seems to be a challenge. We would rather go back to our comfort zone.

I understand. It is easier to go back to your old ways because that is what you are comfortable with. But God is trying to take you to a higher level. But you don't see that, and that's where faith comes in. You must exercise your faith. In the Book of Numbers, as the Israelites were getting to their Promised Land, they sent out some scouts to survey the land (look at it), and they were intimidated by the report or what they saw. Because there were giants already living in the Land— they were big—and, yes, the land was flowing with "milk and honey," as promised. However, the Israelites were intimidated by the giants. They felt miserable and questioned, "Why did the Lord bring us this far for us to be defeated?"

But there were two, Caleb and Joshua, who said, "Wait a minute, if the Lord is faithful to us, He is going to bring us through it." And sometimes, when we get to that point where we can see it, but it seems like a challenge, doubt kicks in and we want to give up and not pursue it. However, we must keep pushing our way, and really, it's the faith. It is the faith that will get you there. That is why faith is very important, it will bring you to that place in life the Lord has for you.

Now you are at that place the Lord has brought you, the Promised Land, and things are all good. You are happy and excited. The Lord has answered your prayers, but then one of two things happens. After a while, the newness wears off and you begin to question where you are and think, *"Is this where I should be?"* Or, you get comfortable in the Promised Land and you begin to neglect or forget where you came from. And that's what happened to the Israelites. The ancestors had died and the new ones did not get to see the deliverance of the Lord to His people. That happens to us, too. We get so caught up in life that we forget God's goodness. The Lord has a way of slowing us down.

Thank God for His grace and mercy.

Other readings:

- Numbers 13: 1–33
- Joshua 14: 6–12
- Proverbs 24: 16

Trust and Contentment

"LORD, my heart is not proud; my eyes are not haughty. I don't concern myself with matters too great or too awesome for me to grasp. Instead, I have calmed and quieted myself, like a weaned child who no longer cries for its mother's milk. Yes, like a weaned child is my soul within me. O Israel, put your hope in the LORD—now and always." Psalm 131 (NLT)

This psalm really helped me when I experienced trouble in my life that I did not quite understand. Sometimes, the cares of this world will try to consume you. Therefore, I literally had to print this scripture out and carry it around with me in my purse. Sometimes, when negative thoughts came to my mind, I recited this psalm, which brought me peace within. And that's what we must do in tough times: carry the Word of God around with us daily. See it and read it.

The psalm states, "I don't concern myself with matters too great or awesome to comprehend." And that's what I had to do: humble myself and stop trying to figure it out on my own. Because I know who is the creator of this universe and who is the author and finisher of my faith. Instead, I quieted my spirit, or calmed myself, to get my thoughts off those things I did not understand.

I knew that God was sitting on the throne even then. I knew I had to give what troubled me to God and quiet my spirit. The psalm concludes, "like a weaned child who no longer cries for his mother's milk." I had this revelation, for me, that God doesn't like crybabies or complainers. So, after a while, I knew I must let it go. I learned that you can't continue to nurse and rehash a situation.

So, I had to stop weeping and let my soul be at peace. An older and wiser lady at my church home in Virginia once told me, "Just rest in God." Quiet and calm yourself. You can't continue to revisit it and try to figure it out. Just trust God and quiet yourself. And eventually, you will get to that point where the cares of this world do not bother you any longer, and you have moved on and let go. Put your hope in the Lord now and always. Amen.

Other reading:

- Hebrews 12: 2–3

This Means War—Don't Let Doubt Creep In

"Finally, my brethren, be strong in the Lord and in the power of His might. Put on the whole armor of God, that you may be able to stand against the wiles of the devil. For we do not wrestle against flesh and blood, but against principalities, against powers, against the rulers of the darkness of this age, against spiritual hosts of wickedness in the heavenly places. Therefore, take up the whole armor of God, that you may be able to withstand in the evil day, and having done all, to stand." Ephesians 6: 10–13 (NKJV)

You must be careful. Some days can be full of joy and some days can be full of darkness. And what has happened? Nothing! Your circumstances around you have not changed. The battle is in your own mind. Therefore, be mindful of spiritual warfare, the devil wrestling within you.

On a particular spring day, out of nowhere, I broke down and cried. I had that moment where I questioned myself. *Am I lying to myself, faking it by having my hopes and promises on His Word? Speaking the Word to everyone, just being on cloud nine, knowing God's Word is true.* Doubt crept in. *What I am doing?* I questioned, *"Is there something in me that the Lord wants me to do?"*

I knew that I had been doing the right thing: staying in the Word. But you know the old saying about the devil, you give him a crack and he will push the door wide open and expose you. And then, you will be crying, saying stuff, like the way I questioned myself, and doubting.

I believe the devil was angry and wanted to shake me because I had been sharing testimonies and greatness with others, talking about God's goodness, and knowing the latter years are better than the former years, saying and speaking the truth and just knowing it. And then I get to that day and just broke down, wondering. I pondered what caused that. I know one thing: You must keep reading His Word, because that is your weapon. I needed to get back to those scriptures that got me full of strength and faith.

So, what I am sharing from this testimony is: Be careful and don't lose hope. Don't let doubt, Satan, or anything creep in to try to knock you off course. When that occurs is when you know you are doing the right thing and your breakthrough is closer than you think. The adversary of this world comes along to ambush you. And this means war! We must stand on it. Gird yourself with the truth, continue to share the good news, and hold up the shield of faith, because the devil will throw fiery darts at you.

And finally, just know that what we go through mentally and spiritually is for our growth. Fight the good fight of faith. Face the challenge, and don't be fearful. God has not given us the spirit of fear.

God is good. Keep the faith and speak it into existence. Thanks be to God!

Other readings:

- 1 Timothy 6: 12
- 2 Timothy 1: 7

Morning Joy, Each Morning: "When You"

"Peace I leave with you, My peace I give to you; not as the world gives do I give to you. Let not your heart be troubled, neither let it be afraid." John 14: 27 (NKJV)

You will find yourself at a place of peace when you can do the following:

- When you don't let the things of the world bother you.

- When you can accept things; whether you're single or married, your past mistakes and mishaps, that stuff is long gone. You are new in Christ.

- When you learn the tools to fight against the enemy, and you can see through people and see how the enemy sends people to set you up.

- When you don't fall into the trap of being torn apart, knowing that the enemy is trying to seek who he can devour, preying upon the weak.

- When you can fight against the enemy.

- When you can stand firm and know the Word of God.

Then you can wake up with morning joy, each morning, and feel good about who you are!

And that's what we are trying to get to. Come to a place of peace, where you know who you are in Christ. It doesn't matter what the world says.

God has sent His son Jesus to die for your sins and mine. The key is maintaining this truth, because sometimes, things will hit you. And that's when you must bounce back, knowing what the Word of God says. When you can bounce back knowing that you trusted, believed, and followed the Word of God, that brings even more joy in your spirit. But when you fall short, become depressed, or fall into the trap of the enemy, that pushes you a step back further, and you are not getting anything accomplished. *I do not want to do that, so I must maintain this continuance of knowing who I am in Christ. Because it feels so good and it gives me confidence, too.* That's how God wants us to be! We also gain testimonies from these experiences to encourage others.

And here is my testimony: I thank God because I recall, a certain period, I was looking good and feeling good and the grace was on me. I had been absorbing myself in the scriptures, trusting and believing. And then what happened months later? I got distracted: I took a new position, taking me temporarily across the country. It was then that I began to watch social media, seeing happy couples, and this and that hit me. It all painted pictures in my mind, including being lonely while on travel status. I got under the weather or depressed, and my spirit was down! And why was my spirit down? Because I accepted the things of this world. You can't go by what you see. Neither can you have one foot in the world and the other in the Word of God. You must stand on

God's Word, despite what you see or how you feel. I began to profess to myself who I am in Christ and cast down those false imaginations. *No, no, accuser of the brethren, God's plan for me is for the good, to give me a future and hope. Praise God! Knowing no weapon formed against me shall prosper.*

Keep the joy! You must profess it! This is the mentality you must maintain while you are in this world. The world will hurt you; the world will curse you. You must put on the whole armor of God. Hallelujah! When you put on the whole armor of God, you can be ready; you can be on the defense when the world attacks you. You can have the spirit of truth, the breastplate of righteousness, you can have all of it, by staying strong in the Lord.

And so, it just feels good and gives you the peace within, a kind of peace that the world cannot give or take away. Amen. Lord, thank you!

Other readings:

- Isaiah 54: 17
- Jeremiah 29: 11
- John 14: 27
- Ephesians 6: 12–18

Turbulence in Life—The Lord Will Calm Your Spirit

And a great windstorm arose, and the waves beat into the boat, so that it was already filling. But He was in the stern, asleep on a pillow. And they awoke Him and said to Him, 'Teacher, do You not care that we are perishing?' Then He arose and rebuked the wind, and said to the sea, 'Peace be still!' And the wind ceased and there was a great calm. Mark 4: 37–39 (NKJV)

When I was on the airplane, traveling to my temporary duty assignment, we experienced gusty winds. The plane was extremely small. I was not really amazed with the initial turbulence because of the size of the airplane, but that little airplane shook me a bit! The wind was moving the airplane back and forth, and it sounded like its wings were flopping, so the only thing I could do was pray. And I meditated on God's Word the entire flight.

As I reflect on this experience, I thought of my home church pastor (Virginia), who once said, "When you can't get to church but when you have the Word of God, a hymn, or song in your spirit that will give you peace." Yes, the plane ride was a horrible experience for me, but when I closed my eyes and meditated on God's Word, "Peace be still," knowing who God is, it instantly gave me peace. It calmed me totally. Stay in the Word, you never know when you will need it.

Glory be to God.

Other reading:

- Luke 8: 22–25

God Rewards, Rid Yourself
of Bad Company

*"Blessed is the man who walks not in the counsel of the ungodly,
nor stands in the path of sinners, nor sits in the seat of the scornful;
but his delight is in the law of the LORD, and in His law he meditates
day and night. He shall be like a tree planted by the rivers of water,
that brings forth its fruit in its season, whose leaf also shall not
wither; and whatever he does shall prosper." Psalm 1: 1–3 (NKJV)*

God rewards those who are obedient. When you push away fleshly
desires and set aside sinful ways because you know they are not good
for you, and it is your desire to please the Lord, God will reward that in
due season. In due time, He will bless you. You must crucify the flesh
and put away those things that are not of God or those things that are
simply in the way (that keep you from getting closer to God). When
you let go of worldly thoughts and behavior and focus on the Lord and
His righteousness, the reward is going to come. And when you see that
reward, you will realize: *Yes, following the Lord and staying on the right
track surely pays off.* The Bible is an instructional manual for our life;
following it leads to a life of peace.

You don't have to follow the ways of the world. Rid yourself of bad
behavior and bad company. Beware of evil people, those who are up

to no good. Be reminded of how a person made you feel. Consider if they truly hurt you, then they may not be for you. [Forgive and move on] God will bring the right people into your life and everything else you desire, once you really put forth the effort and focus on God. After a while, once you keep doing it, it will become part of your life.

Other readings:

- Isaiah 55: 6–9
- 1 Corinthians 15: 33

Hostage Situations and Being in Bondage

*"'And you will know the truth, and the truth will set
you free.' Jesus replied, 'I tell you the truth, everyone
who sins is a slave of sin.'" John 8: 32, 34 (NLT)*

In a training course, Hostage Situations: How to Respond, there are two things learned that I have committed to memory when in a real-life hostage situation. They are:

1. Exercise. Do some form of physical exercise.
2. Keep your faith. You must meditate on good things. You must maintain your faith and keep a good state of mind.

As I meditated on hostage situations from a physical standpoint, I reflected on the lesson from a spiritual perspective. I began to parallel hostage and bondage situations to spiritual warfare. Jesus has already paid the price and won the battle on Calvary, for you and me. We are free; the battle has already been won. However, some of us may still find ourselves in bondage. When you are in spiritual bondage, you can use the same tools the professionals suggest for when you are in physical bondage. Preserving faith will lead you to that breakthrough and will help you to not succumb or go under. To overcome your adversary, the devil, you must keep the faith. Also, maintain a good state of mind, which will require physical activity like going to the gym or using home workout videos. Because sometimes, if the physical body is drained, that is when you are weak, and when you are weak, that's when the enemy can attack. Coupled with not having a good dose of faith, that is you will go under. Be on guard and stay alert, because the adversary, the devil, is prowling around like a lion, preying on the weak (physically, spiritually, and mentally).

And this is so true with my day-to-day activities at work. I work out to have clarity in my mind. I found that when I do work out often and on a continuous basis, I have a clearer mind. I can focus better, and I am oh, so ready for what lies ahead. So, if you find yourself in some form of bondage, it is good to get out and exercise, do something positive to keep you afloat, and stay in God's Word.

To God be the glory for this insight. Amen.

Other reading:

- 1 Peter 5: 8-9

Live to Have a Clear Mind
and a Clear Conscience

But do this in a gentle and respectful way. Keep your conscience clear. Then if people speak against you, they will be ashamed when they see what a good life you live because you belong to Christ. 1 Peter 3: 16 (NLT)

I observed that I can be in my prayer and, while I am in my prayer, I can feel the presence of the Lord and know what I need to do and how to do it. But then, I asked myself one day, *Why is it when you come out of your prayer you seem to forget who you are in Christ?* I forget about what I just prayed about, meaning *Greater is He that is in me, than he that is in the world.* How soon I let the things of this world bother me! I forget that I must have self-control and that I am not going to be moved by the trials and tribulations.

To have a clear mind and a clear conscience—thank you, Lord! You must have that, because if not, the enemy will throw trash into your mind. You will make unwise and ungodly decisions.

We must study the Word, meditate on it day and night. That is the only way this can become a consistent behavior. You must get the Word in your spirit, soul, heart, and mind. Renew your heart and mind in Christ Jesus.

If you are not careful, you can aimlessly drift in this world. You may forget about what the Word of God says. Why? Because you are caught up in the ways of the world. We need to intentionally try to keep our

76

consciences clear, have a focused mind, and maintain our self-control. It happens; we can get so caught up in the world that we forget who we are and lose that righteousness in a matter of seconds. And then, at the end, you have that conviction. Conviction is not a guilty conscience; it is when you are convicted by the Holy Spirit for your sins, and you then turn to repentance and have a relationship with Christ. Know the difference. Otherwise, from my experience, Satan will try to mess with you, condemn you, and make you feel like you are not worthy.

So, as the Word of God says, keep your conscience clear. Then if people speak against you, they will be ashamed when they see what a good life you live because you belong to Christ.

Other readings:

- Joshua 1: 8
- Romans 12: 2

Run the Race of Faith

"Therefore we also, since we are surrounded by so great a cloud of witnesses, let us lay aside every weight, and the sin which so easily ensnares us, and let us run with endurance the race that is set before us, looking unto Jesus, the author and finisher of our faith, who for the joy that was set before Him endured the cross, despising the shame, and has sat down at the right hand of the throne of God. For consider Him who endured such hostility from sinners against Himself, lest you become weary and discouraged in your souls." Hebrews 12: 1–3 (NKJV)

I was reading the Book of Faith—Hebrews, Chapter 12, and it tells us that we have such a great crowd of witnesses of faith. These are the people who had faith, who just did not give up: Abraham, Sarah, and many more faithful believers can be found in the Bible. And then it tells us, to strip off every weight that slows us down, entangles us, especially sin that traps us. Let us run with endurance, the race that God sets before us. We do this by keeping our eyes on Jesus, the author and finisher of our faith.

So, when I think about this, I am reminded that I must run the race; I must keep my mind on Jesus and I must endure all things, having patience in tribulation and rejoicing in hope. As I was thinking, I told myself, *No matter where I am, or who I am with, I must remain in faith to God.*

We must lay aside every dead weight (e.g., bad relationships, bad habits, bad attitudes, whatever it may be) and the sin that so easily entangles us. The devil wants to keep you entangled in a web of confusion. Satan wants to trap you. The Bible says he is roaring around like a lion to see who he can destroy.

The good news is that the Bible warns us about the tricks of the enemy. The Bible tells us that we need to run this race with endurance. We don't give up or give in. How do we do this? We do this by keeping our eyes on Jesus, the author and finisher of our faith. So, no matter what we are going through, no matter what we see, feel, or hear, we must keep our eyes straight ahead on Jesus.

I am reminded, from the Book of Ephesians, that in this world it is not easy. It further states, we do not wrestle against flesh or blood but evil spirits, those fallen angels of the devil. So, I was thinking, "*As soon as we express and give our life to Christ, Satan will do all that he can do to attack our faith—to destroy us and turn us away from Jesus.*" And that is why we will have to endure this battle. Stand strong in faith.

We must remember that Jesus can relate to us because He was both in spirit and human form; He was on this earth just like mankind. This is very important. He endured the cross, disregarding the shame, and now He is sitting on the throne with God.

Hebrews 12: 3 tells us to think about all the hostility Jesus endured from sinful people, then you will not become weary and give up. We all face difficult times. Jesus had to carry His own cross. People spat on Him. People talked about Him; they tried to discredit every good thing He did and said. The same holds true today. People will try to nail you to a cross. They will try to discredit every good thing about you and attempt to portray you as a bad person. Endure that cross, whatever you are carrying. I, too, had to carry my own cross in this harsh world. It was not easy and that is why I say, "Thank you, Jesus, for placing my foot on a firm foundation after a while." God is a Deliverer and a Savior.

Keep the faith. There is so much joy when you have a solid relationship with our Lord and Savior. He will pick you up and raise you from the darkness that seems to be in your life. God gets the glory out of everything that seemed to be evil and will turn it to the good. And I can testify to that! I thank God for my relationship with Him.

As I look back and reflect, God has kept me whole in my darkest days. He kept me in my sleepless nights, "hallelujah!" and no one can come before Him. And I know, because my relationship has grown and I have matured, that the devil will try to attack me. So, I must have discernment. I must discern where I should be and not be, where I should go and not go, who I should hang along with and not hang along with, and what I should say and should not say. You do the same.

Thanks be to God.

Other readings:

- Romans 8: 28
- Ephesians 6: 10–18
- 1 Peter 5: 6–10

Stay in the Word: It Will Save You and You Will Come out on Top

"Look, I am coming soon! Blessed are those who obey the words of prophecy written in this book." Revelation 22: 7 (NLT)

When you go through faith challenges, you must stay in the Word. Because if not, you will hear inner voices and temptations that will cause you to shrink back in your faith. I can tell you some of the inner voices I have heard. I felt them eating at me [troubling thoughts], like they wanted me to lose my mind. That's the devil wanting God's children to lose their faith. But when I was going through it, I kept my mind covered in the Word of God. I believe that is the key; if you don't get anything else, keep your mind covered!

When your faith is being tested, keep pushing, pushing, and pushing. I could have lost it; I could have been overwhelmed. But I did not. I got my mind right. And then I started reading my Bible more about faith. You must, otherwise the enemy will come in like a flood, especially when you are already weak, just like he tried to tempt Jesus when He was in the wilderness, fasting for forty days. The adversary will come in when you are at your weakest.

Pay attention to these words. If you are already troubled or burdened by something, the evil one would love to come in and pour more loads on you, to cause you to worry more and to lose faith. The devil wants to throw you into a mental realm of frustration. Therefore, you must keep your mind covered in the Word of God. When you go through it, when things seem bad, when things seem the worst, the antidote for that is the Word of God.

Now I understand what pastors and preachers have been saying when they say, "stay in the Word of God." I used to think, "*When you go through stuff, it's hard.*" But stay in the Word. It will keep you. You must believe it and speak it in your situation. Read scriptures about it. Faith, faith, faith, that's what I did. I kept my mind saturated in the Word of God. Whatever God's will may be, you also must control your thoughts.

Keep your mind covered. You must stay in the Word, so when situations arise in life, the mind will lean toward the Word of God and not toward the ways of the world. Amen.

Other readings:

- Isaiah 26: 3
- Isaiah 59: 19
- Matthew 4: 1–11

Stay Firm: Agree with God and Stay in Peace

"'For the mountains shall depart and the hills be removed,
but My kindness shall not depart from you, nor shall
My covenant of peace be removed,' says the Lord, who
has mercy on you." Isaiah 54: 10 (NKJV)

When feeling down and out, read God's covenant of peace found in Isaiah, Chapter 54 verses 1 through 17 and Luke, Chapter 21. Specifically, in Luke, Chapter 21 Jesus is speaking of His return and the signs of the end of time. You know when sometimes you get a bad vibe in your spirit that lingers on and eventually causes you to worry, become perplexed about things, or your mind just wanders? I was weighed down for about two days. Then I recognized it and pulled myself back up. By Monday morning, I snapped out of it. I woke up, prayed, and talked to the Lord.

You know, it's so amazing. That is why I always pray to the Lord, "Let me not lie to myself." Because, I thought I needed a Word or direction in how I was feeling. But when I prayed to God and asked Him to give me a Word, I was led to Luke, Chapter 21. I did not understand why I was reading it, but I read the entire chapter. And toward the end of this Word, Jesus spoke: "don't let the cares of this world weigh you down," (verse 34). It spoke to me because my spirit was weighed down for about two days. So, one thing I got from this lesson is that you cannot let the cares of this world weigh you down. Because there is going to come a time, as described in the Bible, when all these things are going to happen, and as Christians, we must be watchful and alert. Because if we cannot handle what is happening in our lives now (i.e., when things happened you immediately get discouraged and lose faith), then how will we be able to stand these last days? Scripture says, let us not grow weary while doing good, for in due season, we shall reap, if we do not lose heart.

When these things that Jesus has spoken of come to pass, are we going to be weak, throw in the towel, and give in? That is my prayer, that we have strength. Jesus says, "pray that you have strength, to withstand the forces of the enemies or the cravings of the world." We must work on our spiritual development and character so that we will be able to stand firm when these times come to pass. We want to be strong to encourage people. And, we can't do that if such little things that are happening now in our life keep us down.

Other readings:

- Psalm 119: 28–29
- Luke 21:36
- Galatians 6: 9–10

Let Go and Give It to Jesus

*"Finally, brethren, whatever things are true, whatever things
are noble, whatever things are just, whatever things are pure,
whatever things are lovely, whatever things are of good report,
if there is any virtue and if there is anything praiseworthy—
meditate on these things. The things which you learned and
received and heard and saw in me, these do, and the God of
peace will be with you." Philippians 4: 8–9 (NKJV)*

It takes more than saying, "I am going to give it to Jesus." Because
consciously you are, but in the subconscious mind, you can easily
pick your burden back up and not even realize it. I have learned to
retrain my thoughts (my mind). The subconscious mind will have you
respond and think based on past experiences, things you have been
taught, whether good or bad. Do you ever wonder why in the conscious
mind you are so clear and adamant about what you are going to do
or not do, and then unknowingly, you respond completely against
what you have clearly thought through? You responded based on the
subconscious mind or your habitually programmed way of thinking
or responding. Romans 12: 2 says be transformed by the renewing of
your mind (i.e., changing the way you think). Therefore, it is important
that we line up our thoughts with the Word of God. We must get deep
in the Word and meditate on it both "day and night," so when events
and circumstances happen, we can respond correctly and remain on
the right path with God.

Learn to meditate on the Word, listen to the Bible through audio books or someone else reading it, and cite positive affirmations to clean up the subconscious mind. The Bible tells us to keep our mind on what is good.

Learn to keep only one thought, and that thought must be lined up with the Word of God. When you have too many thoughts in your mind, it will run you crazy. It creates anxiety, worry, and indecisiveness.

Really, give it to Him spiritually, mentally, and physically. Do not pick it back up when it comes to negative thoughts; instead, cast it down in the name of Jesus. You must put the boundary up and when the bad thought resurfaces, say to yourself, I have given it to God. Ask, "Is this thought a good report and praiseworthy?" If not, let it go.

To unburden yourself and let God handle your burden:

- Pray about it.
- Recall the things the Lord has done for you in the past.
- Anoint whatever it may be, through the action of anointing oil and prayer.
- Trust God!

Other readings:

- Joshua 1: 8
- Ephesians 4: 23

Why I Am Going through This?
This Is all about Faith

"Beloved, do not think it strange concerning the fiery trial which is to try you, as though some strange thing happened to you; but rejoice to the extent that you partake of Christ's sufferings, that when His glory is revealed, you may also be glad with exceeding joy." 1 Peter 4: 12–13 (NKJV)

Maybe you are experiencing these storms back-to-back so that you can increase your faith. This is what you have been praying for, right? You need to learn how to prepare and deal with the storms of life. Why do you fret about strange things happening to you? You are out of control; you have no faith. The Bible speaks of the devil roaring around like a lion to see who he can devour. Stand firm on your faith. Don't be shaken. Yes, the foundation will move, but the Word of God says, "Upon this rock, I build my church and the gates of hell will not prevail." You need to know what the Word says. Remember, we have gone through this already. Yes, you are not alone. You are going from faith to doubt and doubt to faith, back and forth, again and again. Don't let the devil steal your energy because he does not have the victory. Don't have regrets about anything. Move forward in life. Regrets will drain your energy and the enemy will recall things in your past to keep you stagnant or cause you to go back from which you received deliverance.

Other readings:

- Matthew 16: 18
- 1 Peter 5: 8

Move from Faith to Faith

"For I can do everything through Christ, who gives
me strength." Philippians 4:13 (NLT)

Now is the time to move from faith to faith. The following is how to do that.

- Wait on the Lord: be of good courage.
- He is our God and we are His people.
- God wants us to live a prosperous life.
- Develop healthy habits; don't let bad habits stop you. Picture goodness in your life. Your negative thoughts will produce negative things in your life, so let this pattern of thinking go. Keep your mind on whatever is good, worthy of praise, true and good, not evil.
- Despite what you see, have faith. Don't have doubts, as it will work out (again, is anything too impossible for God?).
- God keeps His promises.
- Don't forget what you have read in the Bible and were taught by the pastor. Stay in the right lane.
- God's way is the best and the safest way for you, your life, and your loved ones.
- Don't sway to the left or right. You're reaching for a higher calling. Don't let the bumps take you off the path.

- Move up the mountaintop. This is hard, but put on your hiking gear—the Word of God and prayer.
- Visualize your mountaintop! What's at the top of your mountain? _____
- Don't look back. Looking back will distract you and may take you off balance. Stay focused on every step. Keeping your eyes fixed straight ahead!

Declaration Statement: I am a (wo)man of faith and not a (wo)man of doubt.

Other readings:

- Psalm 27: 14
- Proverbs 4: 25–27
- Matthew 19: 26
- Philippians 4: 8

Anger

*"Understand this, my beloved brothers and sisters. Let everyone
be quick to hear [be a careful, thoughtful listener], slow to speak
[a speaker of carefully chosen words and], slow to anger [patient,
reflective, forgiving]; for the [resentful, deep-seated] anger of
man does not produce the righteousness of God [that standard of
behavior which He requires from us]." James 1: 19–20 (AMP)*

My prayer: "Lord, help us not to focus on the things that will hurt us
or others."

James 1: 19–20 states that the anger of man does not produce the
righteousness of God. We should not focus on things that will cause
conflict or discourse. The Lord loves you. All is well. The Word of God
says, above all things, I want all to be well with you.

Don't let people cause you to get out of character. Just tell them,
"I must continue this conversation later." And don't let them provoke
you after you make this statement (because they will) and say that you
are running.

Just have joy. Galatians, Chapter 5 tells us that the sinful nature
of our flesh brings forth division, anger, and lack of self-control. But
the fruit of the spirit is love, joy, peace, patience, kindness, goodness,
faithfulness, gentleness, and self-control.

Humble yourself. People will know that you know God by your stature and the grace on you. It is all well.

Other readings:

- Galatians 5: 16–23
- 3 John 1: 2

Reassurance

"Therefore whoever hears these sayings of Mine, and does them, I will liken him to a wise man who built his house on the rock: and the rain descended, the floods came, and the winds blew and beat on that house; and it did not fall, for it was founded on the rock." Matthew 7: 24–25 (NKJV)

No matter what you feel, no matter what you see, and no matter how concerned you are about the future, you must trust and believe that your house is built on a solid foundation.

- We must obey God's commands.
- We must listen and follow the Lord's teachings.
- This is the only way to a true happy life.

When we do this, we can have assurance that our house is built on a firm foundation.

Other readings:

- Psalm 119: 1–8
- Psalm 144: 15

Practice Speaking and Living in Faith

"(As it is written, 'I have made you a father of many Nations') in the presence of Him whom he believed—God, who gives life to the dead and calls those things which do not exist as though they did." Romans 4: 17 (NKJV)

Speak of those things that are not as if they are! You are made new in Christ. Everything has been made new. Declare it and believe it!

You must let go of the terrible things that hurt you from the past. Also, let go of the by-products that once were a part of you: worrying, passing judgment, and negative thinking.

Because you have been made new in Christ, you must think of the goodness of the Lord. Speak faithful words of righteousness, edification (uplifting), and practice controlled thinking. Keep your mind on peaceful matters. Have faith, the spirit of truth, joy, and hope for tomorrow. You know the plans God has for you are for the good.

Other readings:

- Jeremiah 29: 11
- 2 Corinthians 5: 17

In This World

"Put on the whole armor of God, that you may be able to stand against the wiles of the devil. For we do not wrestle against flesh and blood, but against principalities, against powers, against the rulers of the darkness of this age, against spiritual hosts of wickedness in the heavenly places. Therefore take up the whole armor of God, that you may be able to withstand in the evil day, and having done all, to stand." Ephesians 6: 11–13 (NKJV)

There is evil in this world, and this is what we call the devil. The devil comes to kill, steal, and destroy. He is a liar and the father of lies. You can't trust him. He is also the prince or ruler of this world. And, because we are in this world, we must put on the whole armor of God (His goodness), so we can stand against the strategies of the evil one. When you wake up in the morning, pray and know this! Because when you wake up, you are in contact with this world and in this world, you will have trouble. Trouble, how? Through people, the customs of this world, and your thought life (internal conflict embedded in your mind from bad life experiences in this world).

How do you stand firm? You stand firm by putting on the whole armor of God. What is the whole armor of God? The whole armor of God is:

- The Word of God
- Knowing the truth
- Righteousness

- Peace
- Faith
- Salvation
- Prayer

Other readings:

- John 8: 44
- John 10: 10
- John 12: 31
- Ephesians 6: 14–18

"This Kind" through Prayer and Fasting

"So Jesus said to them, 'Because of your unbelief; for assuredly, I say to you, if you have faith as a mustard seed, you will say to this mountain, "Move from here to there," and it will move; and nothing will be impossible for you. However, this kind does not go out except by prayer and fasting.'" Matthew 17: 20–21 (NKJV)

You must believe and not doubt. Have faith. The disciples could not heal the little boy who suffered terribly. One hindrance was the disciples' unbelief, and the other is "this kind" (the unclean spirit) goes out by fasting and prayer.

Jesus told the disciples in Matthew 19: 26 that with men it's impossible, but with God all things are possible. This is where we activate our faith and belief system. Jesus has given us a promise that with God all things are possible. In life, we can't grow weary and doubt because of what we see. Keep the faith and you must believe!

Other reading:

- Mark 11: 22–24

Sober-Minded

"Be sober, be vigilant; because your adversary the
devil walks about like a roaring lion, seeking whom
he may devour." 1 Peter 5: 8 (NKJV)

Building up your faith – the process. As I reflect on my faith journey, I realize that I progressed through various stages of faith. In an earlier stage, I learned that I can't trust mankind, I must depend on God wholeheartedly. I learned to keep to myself, and I learned to walk the faith-walk. I put faith into action, trusting, and believing in God. Later, there came a stage that I call being sober-minded (i.e., calm and collected) and vigilant, knowing the favor of the Lord is on my life.

Sober-minded. You must control your thinking. If you can conquer your way of thinking, nothing can conquer you. Not even the adversary, the devil because the mind is renewed.

The Word of God tells us to keep our mind on those things that are good, worthy of praise, excellent, and not evil, mean, and nasty. It tells us to keep our mind on things that are good. You must pursue this way of thinking in every area of your life: your relationship, your job, your home, your community, and so on. This is the pathway to peace.

You must keep your mind on what is good. And I always say to myself, *I am a woman of faith, not doubt.* So, no matter what you see, hear, or feel, be that person of faith. Always think of the goodness, because the Word of God tells us that Jesus came to give us life, and that is life more abundantly. Abundantly can mean so much. You must trust and believe that God's plan for your life is for the good.

Jeremiah 29: 11 reads, "For I know the thoughts that I think toward you, says the Lord, thoughts of peace, and not of evil, to give you a future and a hope." Learn what the Word of God says so the devil will not succeed with deception. You have heard this before; the battle is in the mind. For example, I have experienced sitting in the house becoming very upset about a situation. Continuing to think about the bad led to depression. I have learned that we can bring depression on ourselves by continuing to think about negativity. That is why the Word of God says, keep your mind on what is good, not on what is bad. You may have had something that happened bad in your life; if you sit on the couch and continue to meditate on it, rolling it over and over in your mind and letting the devil continually speak to you, you are giving the devil access to your thoughts about life. The devil will begin to manipulate things and take you on a whole different level: the worst level. Come back! Therefore, you must speak against it with the Word of God. When you don't speak against what you hear or see in the natural, and keep letting the negative thoughts replay in your mind and not replace it with godly thoughts, that will send you into a depression. This may cause you to make the wrong decision or cause you to say or do the wrong thing. Those bad thoughts, those bad suggestions, if they are not checked by renewing your mind daily, you will respond as the way of this world. The Word of God tells us to conform not to the ways of this world but to renew your mind. You must think before you speak and act.

You must conquer your mind, conquer your way of thinking. The mind is one of the most important organs in the body. It tells us what to do, what to say, where to go. Yet, it seems there must be something intangible that controls the mind. The mind is what controls you and your everyday activities: how you respond to folks, what you choose to do and what you choose not to do. However, you can transform your mind for the good. Romans 12: 2 (NLT) reads "Let God transform you into a new person by changing the way you think."

It is the Word of God. Renew your mind by reading and meditating on the Word of God daily.

Keep your mind on things that are good. This is what the Word of God teaches us. God wants what's best for you. You must find it in scripture; the Word truly helps. This is your life. Stay sober-minded, so that you can dodge the fiery darts of the enemy in the name of Jesus (i.e., calm and collected).

Other readings:

- John 10: 10
- Philippians 4: 8

No Devil in Hell

"And war broke out in heaven: Michael and his angels fought with
the dragon; and the dragon and his angels fought, but they did
not prevail, nor was a place found for them in heaven any longer.
So the great dragon was cast out, that serpent of old, called the
Devil and Satan, who deceives the whole world; he was cast to
the earth, and his angels were cast out with him. Then I heard a
loud voice saying in heaven, 'Now salvation, and strength, and
the kingdom of our God, and the power of His Christ have come,
for the accuser of our brethren, who accused them before our God
day and night, has been cast down. And they overcame him by the
blood of the Lamb and by the word of their testimony, and they did
not love their lives to the death.'" Revelation 12: 7–11 (NKJV)

No devil in hell is going to steal my peace, my joy, and my happiness. No devil in hell is going to bother my child, come into my house, and try to rule it. No devil in hell has control of my mind and the things I do.

You must understand this; he (Satan) is the father of lies. You don't have to listen and respond to every thought or suggestion that comes to mind from him. See, he is so cunning and deceiving, he will catch you off guard. If you are not careful, you will fall into his trap. So, if it does not line up with the Word of God, abort it!

We must stand on guard and be alert. The Bible tells us that Satan deceives the whole world. He brought sin on this earth; he could not rule in Heaven, so he wants to make earth his kingdom and turn us away from God. You must know and study the Word so you can be cognizant of this world we live in and who lives in this world among you. Consider that we are the ambassadors on earth, here for the Lord, to spread the good news and make all become aware of our Lord and Savior Jesus Christ. Jesus comes to reconcile us back to our Heavenly Father. We must stay in the Word every day because this world is not our final home.

Other reading:

- Isaiah 14: 12

The Cares of This World:
A True Illustration

"The seed that fell among the thorns represents others who hear God's word, but all too quickly the message is crowded out by the worries of this life, the lure of wealth, and the desire for other things, so no fruit is produced." Mark 4:18–19 (NLT)

Mark, a disciple of Jesus, writes this message. It plagued the disciples back then as it still does today. How easy it is for our daily routines to become so overcrowded that it causes us not to be fruitful for God's kingdom. Stay free so you can hear when God speaks.

So, one day I wasn't feeling right within myself. I began to think and I realized it is the cares of this world that were causing my uneasiness. I became uneasy about my house, and realized that I had been watching a reality TV show with my daughter. And you know, those things of this world—the desires to have certain things—can choke you, blind you from the truth, and you don't receive God's Word. I realized this was the reason why I was so uneasy. My mind was not on God's Word, but on the things of the world.

This is an illustration how God's Word is true. What you experience in life can be found in the Bible. Your answer is found in the Word of God. You must read it, be ready, and stand firm because God's Word is true. The scripture tells us that you can have God's Word in you and immediately the message can fall off because it is choked out by the things of this world. Therefore, you won't receive it. You will get caught up with the things in the world and lose faith in God. I encourage you to stay in God's Word. We must know what the Word of God says, because in this life we will have trials and tribulations. Thank God for His Word, hold on to His Word.

Other readings:

- John 16: 33
- 1 John 2:16

Stay Supercharged with Your Faith

*"And we know [with great confidence] that God [who is deeply
concerned about us] causes all things to work together [as a
plan] for good for those who love God, to those who are called
according to His plan and purpose." Romans 8: 28 (AMP)*

Stay supercharged with your faith. You must believe. (I believe that
God took me through various processes [the faith journey] until I
got it!)

Living in expectancy. Give God praise for where you are right now.
Without a doubt during a particular time of my faith journey, I knew
and believed God was ordering my steps. He brought things to the
surface that I could take care of them, so that in the future I would be
set up for the good. That's how God works: He clears the path.

We do not know the future He has for us. But we do know that He
has promised us the goodness, and every good and perfect gift comes
from above. The Word tells us that God's plans for us are for the good
to give us a future and hope.

Wherever you are in your life, you must truly believe God is
orchestrating things and ordering your steps. You must trust Him: in
Him I will trust. Though at times it is hard, as He brought me to my

knees crying. But I had to pull myself back up and be reminded that His Word says, God is going to shake up things and only the unshakable will remain. We cannot have our faith in our finances or our relationships, it must be in God and His kingdom. And when we seek His kingdom and live righteously, all other things will be added.

Every area of your life must have God first. Lay your finances, relationships, children, job, and all else at His feet.

I can honestly say every area where I have been attacked by the enemy drew me closer to God. I had to muster up more faith and it took many steps of falling and made me realize that I must give it all to God. I tried to do this in my own strength, but that did not work. So, ultimately, God must be the head of every area of my life. And I really trusted and believed on the day of this original meditation: watch how God operates.

At that time, I knew I must do my part and I prayed for His grace and strength to be obedient and faithful and follow His will, because I wanted to see how the end is going to be. I genuinely believed in my heart that God was working all things out for my good, despite how it looked in the natural.

And He did just that! All God's promises are "Yes" and "Amen."

Other readings:

- Psalm 91: 2
- Jeremiah 29: 11
- Matthew 6: 33
- 2 Corinthians 1: 20
- Hebrews 12: 27

Happy New Year: Today Is the Day to Reflect

"Where there is no vision, the people perish: but he that keepeth the law, happy is he." Proverbs 29: 18 (KJV)

Don't lose perspective about anything as you start off the New Year. Think great thoughts. You attract what you think. Move forward knowing that great things are happening in your life right now. You don't see it in the natural realm, but it's happening! You must believe and accept in your spirit that great results are coming your way. Repeat to yourself the great things you want in your life. For example, say, "I have confidence and I am not shaken by what I feel or see in the now." Trust God and lean not to your own understanding. Acknowledge God and He will guide you.

I have been there with mind-boggling thoughts. Change your thoughts, change your life. The Bible says, so what a man thinks in his heart, so is he.

Get a poster board or paper and write down your vision and goals for the year. Visualize it, cut pictures out of a magazine, dream it, do whatever it takes. And post it in a place where you can see it daily. It is your job to believe and God's job to manifest it. With trusting God comes obedience, too. Faith can do amazing things, but it's a journey for each of us.

Without a vision, the people perish. What is your vision for the New Year?

Other readings:

- Proverbs 3: 5–6
- Proverbs 23: 7

Life in the Spirit

"And He said to her, 'Daughter, your faith has made you well. Go in peace, and be healed of your affliction.'" Mark 5: 34 *(NKJV)*

Lamentations 3: 22–24 reads, the Lord is faithful, His love never ends, and each morning there are new mercies, and because of this we have hope in God. Great is His faithfulness.

God sent His son Jesus to die for our sins. There is no condemnation to those who are in Jesus Christ. He will not condemn you. You ask for forgiveness, move on, and go in peace; your faith has made you well. Don't sin again.

And, when the devil tries to throw up thoughts in your mind because you committed past sins, remember what the Word of God says: He forgives us for our sins.

As spiritual and human beings, we must be reminded that the flesh and the spirit are also warring against each other. With our sinful nature, the results are obvious: sexual immorality, lustful pleasures, hostility, jealousy, anger, drunkenness, and the like. Scripture reads living this way, you cannot inherit the Kingdom of God. But the Holy Spirit produces this kind of fruit in our lives: love, joy, peace, patience, kindness, goodness, faithfulness, gentleness, and self-control. When we decide to live in the spirit (Christ), we have nailed our fleshly nature (desires) to the cross and we crucify them there (the flesh). You can't go back. That is my prayer, that we crucify the sinful nature to the cross, live a life in the Spirit, and give the enemy no footstool. We will not have a depressed or saddened state of mind. We will stay focused on the Word of God. Thank you, Lord!

Other readings:

- John 3: 16
- Romans 8: 1
- Galatians 5: 16–25
- Ephesians 4: 27

Do You Want Peace? Meditate on the Word, Day and Night

"Blessed is the man who walks not in the counsel of the ungodly, nor stands in the path of sinners, nor sits in the seat of the scornful; but his delight is in the law of the LORD, and in His law he meditates day and night. He shall be like a tree planted by the rivers of water, that brings forth its fruit in its season, whose leaf also shall not wither; and whatever he does shall prosper." Psalm 1: 1–3 (NKJV)

The Word of God says when you meditate on the Word, you are like a tree planted by the rivers of water, bearing fruit in its season. This psalm brings peace. Think about a tree, planted right on the riverbank. The tree will receive its nutrients from the river, the water. And in due time, it will bear much fruit. The Word says, you will prosper in everything you do. So, when I think about my circumstances, knowing I am meditating and staying in the Word of God and obeying His instructions, I am, in essence, like a tree planted by a riverbank. Even if I don't see fruit, I know God is working on my roots. Sometimes that is how it is: you feel like God is not with you. In your human thinking, you may think that you are not bearing fruit and your leaves are withering away. But that is not what the Word of God says, it says if you meditate on His Word both day and night (habitually) and if you obey His Word, you are going to be like a tree planted along a riverbank bearing much fruit in due season, and you will prosper in everything you do.

You must meditate on God's Word and activate your faith. When going through a tough situation, this is when your faith must kick in. God tells us to keep our mind on what is good. Meditate on His Word. I declare that you will not accept the lies of the enemy that your leaves are withering away (i.e., you are growing day by day in faith and prospering in what you do). It is behind the scenes. It is in your roots. And right now, you can't see your roots. You can't see your roots because of all the dirt and stuff on top. But it is working! Hold on, because when the roots grow and catch on, you will have healthy roots and you will bear much fruit.

This goes along with having those trials and tribulations that come to make you strong and shape your character. This produces perseverance, and you must grow strong roots. Sometimes, we are shaken. But if you have strong roots, you will not be uprooted. You will stand firm on God's Word. You must know that you are prospering in what you are doing and don't grow weary doing good because God is with you, though you may not see it.

Things are happening behind the scenes that you just don't see it in the natural right now. Hold on to faith and don't get discouraged. God is with you; He will never leave you. If you accept the lies of the enemy and go by what you feel and see in the world, you will become discouraged. God says, "Don't be discouraged, I am with you always." Take your eyes off the world and keep them on Jesus Christ. You will have peace.

Other readings:

- Isaiah 41: 10
- Galatians 6: 9
- James 1: 2–4

Live Expecting

"For such a person ought not to think or expect that he will
receive anything [at all] from the Lord, being a double-
minded man, unstable and restless in all his ways [in everything
he thinks, feels, or decides]." James 1: 7—8 (AMP)

Your own thinking can get in your way. Stop putting limits on what the Lord can do. The Word of God specifically tells us to keep our mind on those things that are true, noble, just, pure, lovely, and worthy of praise.

Now as I lay in the bed on that winter morning, I reflected. I recently spoke the Word over my life for the New Year. I professed that this was the year of restoration, manifestation, execution, transformation, and all that is true. However, the day before, I found myself slipping into a repeated cycle based on my way of thinking, not living in expectancy. I recognized such and as I lay in the bed I told myself I must get up each morning knowing it is a new day, with new mercy and new grace. Just talk to God. You cannot have two voices, two thoughts. Have one thought and align it with the Word of God. God's plans for all His children are for the good.

God tells us in His Word that we can have life more abundantly. Sometimes, though, we hurt ourselves with our limited thinking or thinking the worst. So, we must live each day waking up in expectancy. Think big because God is big. He is omnipotent.

The favor of the Lord is on your life, despite what you see and feel. Amen.

Other reading:

- Philippians 4: 8

Soul Anchored

"This hope is a strong and trustworthy anchor for
our souls. It leads us through the curtain into God's
inner sanctuary." Hebrews 6: 19 (NLT)

You must really think! Satan will distract you and have you so focused on the flesh that you don't really think about your soul being anchored in the Lord. And that's what is valuable: your soul anchored in the Lord. No matter what, keep your hope in Jesus Christ. This hope will sustain us.

I read an article and it says two things will last forever: The Word of God and people. I believe we should build an intimate relationship with God first, where we talk to Him every day, where you are concerned about His will for your life. It is my prayer that we help our souls to be anchored in the Lord. He is the source of our strength and we should rely on Him daily for everything.

Know that God has given us everything we need to live a godly life. He has given us His promises, so that we can escape the corruption of the world. Keep your mind on the promises of God so that when situations hit you in life, you can reflect on His promises (e.g., by His stripes I am healed, Greater is He that is in me than He that is in the world). Confess His Word over your life; confess His Word over situations and events that you go through. We must keep our hope in Christ Jesus.

Other readings:

- Isaiah 53: 5
- 2 Peter 1: 3–8
- 1 John 4: 4

Love

"If I could speak all the languages of earth and of angels, but didn't love others, I would only be a noisy gong or a clanging cymbal. If I had the gift of prophecy, and if I understood all of God's secret plans and possessed all knowledge, and if I had such faith that I could move mountains, but didn't love others, I would be nothing. If I gave everything I have to the poor and even sacrificed my body, I could boast about it; but if I didn't love others, I would have gained nothing." 1 Corinthians 13: 1—3 (NLT)

I was convicted. I did not have peace in my house. So, I searched the scriptures to get help. You know that sometimes you must search and find scriptures that speak to your circumstances. Once you find that Word, you must study it and meditate on it, like you are going to school. You must get the Word deep down into your soul, mind, and spirit because you need the change for the good.

I was reading about being critical and judgmental. And I was thinking, *"That was me. I can be overly critical sometimes."* During this period of my faith journey, I would think the worst, not giving anyone the opportunity for the good. (Thank God, I have been delivered.)

The Bible asks, "How can you be judgmental when you have a speck in your own eye?" First, get the speck out of your own eye before you judge someone else. God is the final judger, not us. We cannot go around condemning people for what they have done. And judgment per Webster's dictionary is defined as to condemn, to pass over an opinion based on what somebody has done, and it also says, to sentence. I thought, *"That's really tough!"*

God has mercy on us, so we should have mercy on others and not judge people. God is love, and love is the greatest. The Bible says there are three things that last forever: faith, hope, and love, and the greatest is love. And that is so true, because love endures forever.

Love is patient and kind. Love is not jealous, boastful, proud, or rude. It does not demand its own way, it is not irritable, and it keeps no record of being wronged. It does not rejoice about injustice, but rejoices whenever the truth wins. Love never gives up and never loses faith. It is always hopeful and endures through every circumstance. (1 Corinthians 13: 4–8)

If you have love in you, you can't be rude. God is love. You must exhibit Christian behavior. You must be patient and kind, as love is. And you cannot demand your own way, as that's part of that spirit of being judgmental and critical. Keep in mind, what works for you may not work for somebody else, so you cannot demand your own way. You can't get irritated because of what somebody does or if people do not see your point of view. Love keeps no record of being wronged. You see, sometimes, we pass judgment on others because we harbor what they have done to us. And finally, love rejoices whenever the truth wins, and love never gives up. Despite how you feel, how the situation is, love never gives up. Never give up on children, spouse, and family. Love never loses faith; it is always hopeful and endures circumstances. And in every circumstance, you must endure it and always be hopeful. Love hopes for the best.

Other readings:

- Matthew 7: 1–5
- 1 Corinthians 13: 13
- 1 John 4: 8

Reaching Out to the Community

"'People and animals alike must wear garments of mourning, and everyone must pray earnestly to God. They must turn from their evil ways and stop all their violence. Who can tell? Perhaps even yet God will change his mind and hold back his fierce anger from destroying us.' When God saw what they had done and how they had put a stop to their evil ways, he changed his mind and did not carry out the destruction he had threatened." Jonah 3: 8–10 (NLT)

As I continue to read the Book of Jonah, Chapter 3, it highlights the spiritual needs of the community and the mercy of God, as well as how God extends His love to all mankind.

Jonah went to speak to the people in the city of Nineveh. He went to share a message from God that the city would be destroyed if they did not turn from their evil ways. The message was: You will be overthrown in forty days if you do not turn from your ways. But God, He saw their works. He saw that they turned from their evil ways. God did not bring the disaster that He said He would bring upon them. He did not do it! God is so merciful.

God has grace and mercy on us today, as He had grace and mercy on the people of Nineveh. The people listened to God, obeyed God, and turned from their evil ways. Nothing has changed today. People are stuck in their own evil ways, and so the same message must get out to the community.

I began to focus on my childhood community. If the city would turn away from evil, repent, and go to God, oh what joy this would be in the community. It reminds me of 2 Chronicles 7: 14 (NKJV) that says "if My people who are called by My name will humble themselves, and pray and seek My face, and turn from their wicked ways, then I will hear from heaven, and will forgive their sin and heal their land." Can you imagine that is truly heaven on earth, as I visualized it, if God showed up in the entire community and every one can see this miraculous change in the city (no more killings, drug abuse, hatred, etc.) because the people turned away from their evil ways as a whole community?

We must get the word out, share the Good News as a community of believers, if we could grab hold of everybody, if we can grab hold of others that are not in the church and if we can get everybody on one accord. Just knowing how God's Word is so true, He can heal the land and He forgives sin. There is a spiritual need out there; there are many lost souls. Continue to do the work while it can be done.

Other reading:

- John 9: 4

Knowing Who God Is

*"So he said to them, 'I am a Hebrew; and I fear the L*ORD*, the God of heaven, who made the sea and the dry land.'" Jonah 1: 9 (NKJV)*

Through this reading of the Word, the Spirit spoke to me with a confirmation of how life is. There were some mariners on a boat with Jonah, and a great storm came up because of Jonah, who was trying to flee from the presence of the Lord. So, he got on a boat trying to run from God. But once the boat had sailed, a great storm came up. The mariners were afraid and initially prayed to their gods (lower-case g). In the midst of this storm, they realized Jonah was running from the presence of the Lord. And he told them he was a Hebrew and who his God is (the God of the Heaven, who made the sea and the land). From this, the mariners became horrified and scared. Now Jonah told them to throw him into the sea and the sea would be calm. But they did not; instead, they tried to fight against the storm themselves (which did not work), so eventually they threw Jonah into the sea and they prayed to God (capital G). As soon as they threw Jonah into the sea, the sea calmed and the water was calm. From this experience, the mariners feared the Lord and offered a sacrifice to Him and vowed to serve Him.

What I get from this, as this has happened in my life, sometimes, the Lord may speak to us and we don't listen. And it is not until that horrific experience in our lives that we learn to fear the Lord. Listen to God. I recall a man in Bible study years ago at my home church in Virginia, and he said, "Sometimes we can't grow closer to the Lord until we experience something terrible in our life, because it is that terrible thing that will draw us to the cross."

Other reading:

- Jonah 1: 1–16

Thinking too Far into the Future

"'For My thoughts are not your thoughts, nor are your ways My ways,' says the Lord. 'For as the heavens are higher than the earth, so are My ways higher than your ways, and My thoughts than your thoughts.'" Isaiah 55: 8–9 (NKJV)

Our thinking process can only go so far. Sometimes I catch myself, as my imagination tends to run and go far too deeply, trying to think about the future with limited knowledge. As a result, I have, and have tried to, make decisions based on this limited knowledge, not factoring in Jesus the Lord, who can do anything and still work miracles today. Have you been there? Have you had to catch yourself as well?

When I was planning to sell my house, I thought up a scenario in my mind. Step one, this will happen. Step two, that will happen. And then, I got really deep down the road with my thinking. At this point, I was overthinking. *Wait a minute, stop!* I had to stop and slow this mental exercise down. I had to stop and catch myself. I realized I was painting a picture in my mind about stuff, which I did not know the future was going to hold or how God would change things around for me.

Based on past experiences, I know how the Lord can step right in and turn things around. So, I had to stop, because I was looking too far into the future, bringing more anxiety on myself. (We can create our own anxiety by overthinking or overprocessing our thoughts.) I realized this way of thinking was counterproductive, and went back to the Word of God, which reminds me that all things are possible through Jesus Christ.

I also come to realize that sometimes all of that daydreaming and imagination will be based on the now: what your thoughts are now, what your circumstances look like now. So, if this sounds familiar, stop sabotaging your future with limited knowledge. You don't know what God can do. Sometimes you just have to cut it off. And know the Lord will work it out and trust in God. And in the end, my house was sold in ninety days, and I sold it by myself, without a realtor.

God knows the future, not man!

Other reading:

- Matthew 19: 26

Preserving Faith: Faith-Growing Exercise

"And you will be hated by all for My name's sake. But he who endures to the end shall be saved." Mark 13: 13 (NKJV)

Do you ask, "Why, why? What is it that I need to find out? What lesson do I need to learn from this, as a child of God?" The answer is faith. It's all about faith and trusting God.

How do you trust God? You must have faith, trust, and belief, and endure to the end.

As I was growing in faith, I realized I kept having what I call faith-growing exercises. I repeatedly went through the same faith-growing exercises until I got it. These faith-growing exercises were events in my life where I had to ultimately learn to trust God and not get overwhelmed by what I see, feel, or hear in the natural. If I panicked and got bent out of shape or became fearful, I failed the test. But when I trusted the Almighty God despite what I saw, felt, or heard, I passed the test. These little faith exercises or faith challenges were designed to make me strong, so that, when the time comes, I will be able to keep strong and stand strong. The Word of God says, "...Unless your faith is firm, I cannot make you stand firm." (Isaiah 7: 9 NLT)

Our faith can be challenged and opposed by what we are surrounded by and the company we keep. My faith has been challenged, and at times, I felt like I was going in circles. I asked, "Why?" And what I found out is that I need to learn to wholeheartedly trust God. And just give it all to Him, the author and finisher of my faith. As I said before, you will keep experiencing the same thing spiritually until you get it!

It's part of the process, increasing that faith muscle. It's faith and it's supernatural. You must believe. You cannot go by what you see, feel, or hear. The answer is let it go and give it to God, have faith. Endure to the end and be blessed! Keep your mind on what is good and worthy of praise.

Other readings:

- Hebrews 12: 2
- James 1: 2–4

The Gift of Life and Living Well

"Every good gift and every perfect gift is from above, and comes down from the Father of lights, with whom there is no variation or shadow of turning." James 1: 17 (NKJV)

God blessed us with the gift of life. It is up to us to live this life well. Though it sounds so simple and obvious, it is hard for some to do. Why? Because we are constantly battling the things of this world.

But wait, there is hope! How do you give yourself the gift of living well? Well, I would first say to have a relationship with God. Stay in His Word, so He can lead and guide you through life's difficult circumstances. Things come in life that will cause us to be distracted and get off course. It could cause us to divert our attention to those things that are not good for us. We are constantly fighting this battle, and the weak will give up or give in to the difficult circumstances of life.

Every good and perfect gift comes from above. We must change our perspective, no matter what circumstances come our way. The Word of God says, He will not put more on us than we can bear. Those tough circumstances of life come to make us a better and stronger person, and for us to be a blessing in someone else's life. Just spoken words of kindness based on one's experiences can encourage someone. Share the gift of your life. Do good and live right. Live well, love hard, laugh always, and encourage many!

Life is full of blessings in disguise; choose to live your life very well. And, yes, you can, despite how things appear! Stay hopeful and have faith.

Other readings:

- Deuteronomy 6: 18
- 1 Corinthians 10: 13
- Galatians 6: 9

My Hope Is in the Lord

"Blessed is the man who trusts in the Lord, and whose hope is the Lord. For he shall be like a tree planted by the waters, which spreads out its roots by the river, and will not fear when heat comes; but its leaf will be green, and will not be anxious in the year of drought, nor will cease from yielding fruit." Jeremiah 17: 7–8 (NKJV)

When you know that you know, without a shadow of doubt, that you trust the Lord and have confidence in Him and His Word, no matter what you experience in life, you will be okay.

Vividly think of a tree planted by a riverbank. It will have all the nutrients it needs to flourish and to grow green leaves and fruit. (The river is the source of the tree.) The tree grows stronger by the river; it spreads its roots and gets rooted. It does not worry about heat or drought season.

Likewise, when the heat of life comes, you will have all the nutrients that you need. (The Lord is the source of your strength.) Life may throw you a curve ball, but if you trust in the Lord and your hope remains in the Lord, you will have all you need to continue to produce good fruit and will not fear. Second, in life, your resources may dry up, or what is going on in the physical realm seems like there is no way out and may cause you to want to lose hope. But wait, the Word says, even in drought season you don't become anxious and you will continue to yield fruit. This is when your unchanging hope and trust must kick in. Stay focused on God and His Word, and not the problem. Your life is truly blessed.

Other reading:

- Nehemiah 8: 10

Don't Forget Your Deliverance— Don't Fall Back, Trust in God

"Trust in the Lord with all thine heart; and lean not unto thine own understanding. In all thy ways acknowledge Him, and He shall direct thy paths." Proverbs 3: 5–6 (KJV)

How history repeats itself! God delivers us out of our own personal Egypt (bondage). Things are going well. We are excited about our deliverance. The dust settles, and then what? You begin to worry or your thoughts begin to race. You don't hear from God for a moment. You don't know what your next step is. So, you take matters into your own hands. We forget so quickly about the deliverance. Don't rebel or be stubborn. Hang in there, don't throw in the towel. Stick with God, and He will be with you to take you into the next level in your life.

With wisdom comes good judgment. Leave your simple ways behind and begin to live. Learn how to make good judgments. But how? "Fear of the Lord is the foundation of wisdom. Knowledge of the Holy One results in good judgment." Proverbs 9: 10 (NLT)

Other readings:

- Proverbs 8: 12
- Proverbs 9: 1–12

Hang in There

*"My brethren, count it all joy when you fall into various trials,
knowing that the testing of your faith produces patience. But
let patience have its perfect work, that you may be perfect
and complete, lacking nothing." James 1: 2–4 (NKJV)*

Yes, my obedience has been tested during these storms (the various trials of life). My flesh or the tempter (the adversary) whispered in my ear: go back, do this, do that, hang out. But I counted the cost, and I said "No." At times, I became very weak, crying day and night, wondering, reading the Word, doubting, depressed, and then I was faithful again. But then I said, "Lord, give me strength; I do not want to be up and down. Please increase my faith." Now I believe these storms occurring back-to-back in my life were testing my faith, as the scripture reads.

I have heard it repeatedly: Remain faithful and obedient to God and you will see the blessings in your life. The blessing of the Lord makes one rich and adds no sorrow. (Proverbs 10: 22)

Other reading:

- Luke 17: 5

We Are in Control of Our Life, Choose How to Live It

"Today I have given you the choice between life and death, between blessings and curses. Now I call on heaven and earth to witness the choice you make. Oh, that you would choose life, so that you and your descendants might live!" Deuteronomy 30: 19 (NLT)

We are in control of our life. Just think about it. Really, after the age of twenty-one, you don't have professors or parents guiding you or telling you what to do step by step. It's now your life and you are responsible for the decisions you make. You are now in control of your life.

Life is a period of time given to us by the Almighty God. And we must utilize this time to the best of our ability, whether good or bad. The choice is yours. No one knows the end of his or her life. Life comprises years, months, weeks, days, hours, minutes, and seconds. So today, on this day, choose how you will live your life. Are there any goals you are trying to achieve? Or are you getting up every day and drifting aimlessly through life?

God has given us the gift of life. How we live this life is up to us.

Other reading:

- Ecclesiastes 12: 13–14

I Encourage You, and You Have Been Here Before

"You must warn each other every day, while it is still 'today,'
so that none of you will be deceived by sin and hardened
against God. For if we are faithful to the end, trusting God
just as firmly as when we first believed, we will share in all
that belongs to Christ." Hebrews 3: 13–14 (NLT)

Life happens. Circumstances in life will come and go. And at times, fear and anxiety will try to take over. You get distracted and forget who you are in Christ. Don't let Satan continue to ambush you with fear or regret. You must have faith continuously and know who you are in Christ. This is nothing different than any other crossroad you have ever taken. Don't get overwhelmed, stay in Christ.

Look fear in the eye and know who you are in Christ. You must get that in your spirit! So, when situations in life come, you will be unmovable. And that is what the Word of God says, He is going to shake the heavens and the earth, and what remains are those who know the Word of God, the unshakable. You must decide that you will be the unshakable one. And you will stand firm on the Word.

We, all of us, are only here for a moment. So why get so wrapped up with the issues of this world, which can cause undue aches and pains in your body (health issues), emotional distress, and stress. The body is the temple of the Lord. You are here momentarily, and the Lord said,

"He will give you an abundant life." So, enjoy life now, today. Things will come and try to shake you, but you have to say, "I am enjoying my life." You must walk in obedience and trust God. And when you are trusting God, walking in obedience, and standing firm, the gates of heaven will open.

This is nothing new; you have been here before. The scripture reads, "For I can do everything through Christ, who gives me strength" (Philippians 4: 13 NLT). Stop taking your soul and body through an emotional roller coaster and stand firm on His Word. Stop being pulled to and fro based on every significant or unexpected event in life. Don't be shaken. Stand firm. You are flexible as palm trees; you can bend. You have already done this before, it's just a different life circumstance or event. It's your perspective.

Life is life, though the circumstance or the experience may be different each time: job concerns, health challenges, marital concerns, bad talks, heartbreaks, and so on. It's life, and you will grow from it. These uncertain or unexpected life events will hit those same trigger points. They all will attack you the same way, meaning your mind may begin to race, your emotions get involved, anxiety kicks in, followed by fear and worry. Stop it, don't let it process. You see it. You have been here before, it's just a different life experience. You already know where this will lead you. So therefore, turn it off, trust in God, and lean not to your own understanding.

The circumstances may be in the physical realm but may attack you also from the spiritual realm. The devil wants you to think the worst of a situation. But wait. You have done this before; you are familiar with this. And since you are familiar with this or the process of how this typically evolves, you must trust God and don't get so involved in the problem. Don't let it engulf you. And that is what I mean when I say that you have been here before. It's a part of life's journey. Things will come in your life that will discourage you, but you must stand firm and trust God. You must put on the whole armor of God and say, "I got this!" You have the shield of faith, knowing that God has not given you the spirit of fear or intimidation. God is a provider and provides rewards to those who diligently seek Him. Walk in His ways and know that He is with you.

Just declare it. It is faith. Everything is built on trusting and having faith in God. And we must learn how to define those categories the devil tries to box us in. And remember, it can be your perception or perspective too. The Word of God says keep your mind on what is good. Pray to Him with thanksgiving and supplication. He will give you all you need. The Lord is a provider. We must call those things that are not as if they are! Thank God for preparing you.

Other readings:

- Proverbs 3: 5
- Romans 4: 17
- Ephesians 6: 11–18
- Philippians 4: 6–8
- 2 Timothy 1: 7
- Hebrews 12: 25–29

A Christian Journey

"The LORD is my shepherd; I shall not want. He makes me to lie down in green pastures; He leads me beside the still waters. He restores my soul; He leads me in the paths of righteousness for His name's sake. Yea, though I walk through the valley of the shadow of death, I will fear no evil; for You are with me; Your rod and Your staff, they comfort me. You prepare a table before me in the presence of my enemies; You anoint my head with oil; my cup runs over. Surely goodness and mercy shall follow me all the days of my life; and I will dwell in the house of the LORD forever." Psalm 23: 1—6 (NKJV)

This Christian journey is hard; it takes a lot, I thought to myself one night after feeling discouraged. You have a spiritual victory, and then it seems like you fall off and become distressed. Because you are a woman of God, it appears that you have many spiritual challenges and must mentally try to focus on the goodness of God, no matter what you are going through. You then must also block out the voice of the enemy: whispering lies, and, sometimes, the lies you thought you had defeated. This can cause a mental and physical drain. But now I realize, this is all part of my Christian journey. With every trial, there comes a test. I read Psalm 23 and thought, *"This psalm illustrates the Christian journey."* Follow me.

"The Lord is my Shepherd. I shall not want." No matter what I am going through, I must believe that scripture wholeheartedly and know that He is my guide. He is my provider.

"He makes me to lie down in green pastures; He leads me beside still waters; He restores my soul. He leads me in the paths of righteousness, for His name's sake." I am saved and redeemed. He helps me to do what is right and good. He forgives and gives peace.

"Yea, though I walk through the valley of the shadow of death." Dark periods of my life that brings hurt, disappointment, betrayal, loneliness, bad thoughts, and hardships, "I will fear no evil. For You are with me. Your rod and Your staff, they comfort me." Even when walking in the valley of darkness, I will not fear evil. God is with me, He and His angels. As I look back, He has walked with me and gave me peace. So even after these dark experiences, I have faith. Don't give up on this. God keeps His promises. This is the faith test.

And once it's all said and done: "He prepares a table before me in the presence of my enemies; and anoints my head with oil and my cup runs over." Blessings.

And finally: "Surely goodness and mercy shall follow me all the days of my life and I will dwell in the house of the Lord Forever." Trusting and believing always.

As part of your faith journey, recognize where you are in the Psalm 23 scripture:

- He is my shepherd (Believe He will guide you)
- Green pastures and still waters (Know He gives you peace)
- Restoration and righteousness (Know He saves and redeems)
- Dark valley and fear not (Know He is with you and will comfort you)

- Goodness and mercy (The Lord will take care of you, wait on the Lord)

Other reading:

- Psalm 91: 1–16

Decision-Making: Scared to Move Forward

"God is our refuge and strength, a very present help in trouble. Therefore we will not fear, even though the earth be removed, and though the mountains be carried into the midst of the sea; though its waters roar and be troubled, though the mountains shake with its swelling." Psalm 46: 1–3 (NKJV)

Know that God is our refuge and He is our strength. We can be scrolling through life, living in peace, and then there is a shakeup. Do you fear and revert to mediocrity (the safety zone) during this time of trouble? No, you continue to stand on God's Word. God's plan for you is for the good. He is your refuge and a very present help in the time of trouble.

Sometimes, we pray and we pray, asking God for the answer to help us make a decision, and sometimes, we already have the spiritual resources in us through faith. Keep in mind that God may not in all times give us an extraordinary sign, pointing us to turn right or left, particularly during times of trouble or uncertainty. It's really based on your belief. Who or what do you trust in? If things are working out for the most part and things line up with God's Word, go for it. However, unexpected things in life can happen and you wonder or question your initial decision. Sometimes this is legitimate. But if your decision pool is made up of doubt, fear, and worry, this is not of God and will lead to ineffective decision-making. When you are scared to make a decision due to worry, doubt, or fear, know that God has called us to walk by faith and not by sight or by fear. God has not given us the spirit of fear. So how do you move forward? Yes, continue to pray and recognize the fear, doubt, and worry. Don't let fear, doubt, or worry drive you or your decision.

Other readings:

- Jeremiah 29: 11
- 2 Corinthians 5: 7
- 2 Timothy 1: 7

Backyard Vision, Clear Blue Sky

"I will lift up my eyes to the hills—from whence comes
my help? My help comes from the LORD, who made
heaven and earth." Psalm 121: 1–2 (NKJV)

I love mother nature's landscaping. A creek ends in my backyard, which includes some marshy land along with tall beautiful trees. I love this view, because as I look at the tall trees it takes my eyes up to the sky, which gives me peace.

This winter day, as I cast my eyes upon the trees and up to the sky, the sky was gray, but I observed between two branches clear, blue sky. It made me think of a blue-sky analogy; the calmness of the brain is like the blue sky. The natural state of the mind is calm, but it can get cloudy due to uncontrollable thoughts. A blue sky represents a beautiful sunny, day with fluffy white clouds (i.e., calmness, happiness, and peace within); conversely, a gray sky represents rain, an overcast, gloom day (i.e., chaos, moody, no peace within). So, I said, "Thank you, God," as I reflected and saw a bit of blue sky amidst the gray.

This vision just reminds me of life in general: No matter what it looks like, there is always a blue sky. And eventually that blue sky will clear the way and everything that was once gray will be blue; what is dark will eventually turn to light. The Word of God says, weeping may endure by night, but joy comes in the morning. That morning joy is your blue sky. The blue sky represents joy, peace, and harmony, but you must move out the cloudiness, because there is something good in everything!

Other reading:

- Psalm 121: 1–8

We Are Overcomers

*"I have told you all this so that you may have peace in me. Here
on earth you will have many trials and sorrows. But take heart,
because I have overcome the world." John 16: 33 (NLT)*

Jesus said to the disciples, "I told you this so that you will have peace in me; on this earth, you have trials and tribulations, but be of good cheer, because I have overcome the world." As I meditate on the Word, it puts a smile on my face because Jesus overcame the world and we can have peace in Him, the overcomer, no matter what we face.

Jesus has already prepared you with His spoken words, so when things happen in life, it should not shake us to the point whereas we lose all hope. Jesus said there will be trials and tribulations on this earth. So, we know it's going to happen, but we do not know when. So, we need to prepare ourselves and we prepare ourselves by standing on a solid foundation, putting our hope and trust in God. We must have faith within and operate in that authority. We can rest in Him and have peace in Him, as the Word says. We are overcomers!

Other readings:

- Luke 10: 19
- 1 John 5: 4–5

My Suffering Was for the Good

"Thus speaks the Lord God of Israel saying, 'Write in a book for yourself all the words that I have spoken to you.'" Jeremiah 30: 2 (NKJV)

My suffering, my writings, and my audio recordings made me more conscientious and more spiritual. I came to know God better through His Word.

My suffering served as an illustration of the Word of God, because if it had not been for my suffering, I may have not drawn closer to the Lord.

My suffering showed me the Word. I was able to connect what I was going through back to the scriptures: the consequences and the faith.

My suffering was for the good, and I thank God because I would not be the person I am today.

In life, you must take a moment and ask, *"What is my purpose?"* And I believe my purpose is to encourage others. Without my trials and tribulations, I could not have encouraged. I recall an old saying that "My suffering is for someone else's blessing or breakthrough." Truly, someone's suffering was for my breakthrough, to help me get through and to know that it will be okay and trust God. My writings, *Journals of Faith*, is to help someone else get through and to encourage others in God's Word. To God be the glory.

Other readings:

- Psalm 119: 71
- 2 Corinthians 1: 3–4
- James 1: 2–4

Prayer

"That if you confess with your mouth the Lord Jesus and
believe in your heart that God has raised Him from the
dead, you will be saved." Romans 10: 9 (NKJV)

Romans 3: 23 says we all sinned and fall short of God's glory. "If we confess our sins, He is faithful and just to forgive us our sins and to cleanse us from all unrighteousness." 1 John 1: 9 (NKJV)

Dear Heavenly Father,

It is written in Your Word that if I confess with my mouth that Jesus is Lord and believe in my heart that You have raised Him from the dead, I shall be saved. Therefore, Heavenly Father, I confess that Jesus is my Lord. I make Him Lord of my life right now. I believe in my heart that You raised Jesus from the dead.

Thank you, Lord Jesus, for dying on the cross for my sins. Please forgive me for my sins. Come into my life. I receive You as my Lord and Savior. Now, help me to live for You the rest of this life. In the name of Jesus, I pray. Amen.